Celtic Wise Woman

Dilys Gater is a practising psychic, medium and Reiki healer. She is the author of the successful *A Psychic's Casebook* and *Past Lives: Case Histories of Previous Existence* (both published by Robert Hale) and has written award-winning plays. She has worked in publishing, journalism, broadcasting and recording. Dilys Gater was born in North Wales and now lives in Newcastle-under-Lyme.

By the same author

A Psychic's Casebook
Past Lives

To Pam
You can !!

Celtic Wise Woman

The Secrets Revealed

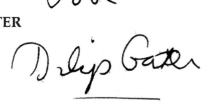

love

DILYS GATER

Dilys Gater

ROBERT HALE · LONDON

© *Dilys Gater 1998*
First published in Great Britain 1998

ISBN 0 7090 6066 1

Robert Hale Limited
Clerkenwell House
Clerkenwell Green
London EC1R 0HT

2 4 6 8 10 9 7 5 3 1

Photoset in North Wales by
Derek Doyle & Associates, Mold, Flintshire.
Printed in Great Britain by
St Edmundsbury Press Limited, Bury St Edmunds
and bound by
WBC Book Manufacturers Limited, Bridgend

Contents

Winter and thick snow
out in the Wilderness,
You are a Wise Woman, and you are kneeling down
picking berries,
You've got a staff, you're wearing purple,
Your hair hangs below your waist.

Amelia Summerfield, Reiki Master, to Dilys Gater
describing images from past existence seen during a
healing session

I fy nghariad arglwydd
PAUL GATER
yn yr enw Apollo Belenos, golau a thân,
yn ôl Brother Gregory
Heb ddiwedd, yn dy garu du

Preface

This book is filled with magic, spells, wisdom and thoughts. But because it is written by a Celtic Wise Woman, this does not mean they are strictly Celtic, or representative solely of Celtic beliefs and the Celtic religion.

In my work as a psychic, medium, counsellor and healer, I employ all the methods that seem to present themselves at any given time in order to communicate on all levels with my sitters, and provide the help, comfort, or whatever else they seem to need. From the wisdom and beliefs of all religions, from the Bible to Nietzsche, from the various Books of the Dead to Jung, from the language of the flowers to the setting of goals and use of affirmations – all is the same truth. So the enlightened in any time or place realize that they go to a common source – and I have included in these pages all kinds of spells and magic, with no restriction on whether they are pagan, Christian, Wiccan, Tibetan, Japanese Buddhist or anything else.

Case histories are included in order to illustrate the points I want to make, and as in my previous books, *A Psychic's Casebook* and *Past Lives: Case Histories of Previous Existence* these are all specific and genuine, though names have been changed to protect my sitters.

My thoughts and opinions do, however, come from a lifetime of Celtic awareness of the shadowy worlds which exist alongside our own, and of sharing in the mysteries – those which are found in secret springs and on the bare, silent summits of mountains, in the depths of thickly wooded ravines and the pale flowers of the ivy, wreathed with the wild rose. Jagged slashes in the richly glowing fabric of the ancient world provided me with a gap through which to slip as a child into those beautiful, dangerous realms – and once I had found the way, I knew the power of the enchantment, and I could never return.

Dilys Gater

Acknowledgements

With grateful thanks and appreciation to the authors of all the works I have consulted as a background for the writing of this book. To all who have come to me for help, and those with whom I have exchanged ideas, who have given me so much. And for their expertise, assistance, interest, energies, particularly to: Louis Rawlings at the University of Wales, Cardiff; Steve Wilson of the Druid Clan of Dana; Gareth J. Medway, Priest of Themis; Geraldine Edmonds, in the tradition of the White Witch; Amelia Summerfield, Reiki Master; Richard Lawler, Psychic and Astrologer, Initiate – *Legend of the Witches* (Border Films), friend and Aquarian.

The extract from the anonymous thirteenth century MS, translated by Ifor Williams, which appears on page 169, is included by kind permission of The Governing Board of the School of Celtic Studies of the Dublin Institute for Advanced Studies.

With thanks to Micola Nevile and to Alison and Marnie at 'MOON', North End Road, for tea and sympathy; to Maroulla for helping me to stay young; to Aimi (Amelia Summerfield) for healing, sharing thoughts, and for recognizing me; to Rosemarie for helping me keep my feet on the ground. To my brother and sister-in-law, David and Irene Binnion in Wrexham, North Wales, for being there with support and for being proud of me. For the Lehanes, Anna,

Mary, Frank, Maura and Sarah, and all the people who welcomed me to Lahinch, County Clare, when I arrived in Ireland alone and ill, following the guidance of the spirits into the west. To Agnes O'Brien in Ennis, who gave me practical help, and to all the others I met on that beautiful Atlantic coast, including the presenter and producers at Clare FM.

Much of the goddess text given in this book has previously appeared in *Wisdom of the Goddess* (anecdotes, 1993) and on cassette as *The Goddess Experience*.

1

Out of the Mist

Ar lan y môr mae carreg wastad,
Lle bûm yn siarad gair â'm cariad;
O amgylch hon mae'r teim yn tyfu,
Ac ambell sbrigyn o rosmari.

On the sea-shore there is a level stone
And there I have been to talk with my darling
All round about it the thyme grows
And a few sprigs of rosemary.

A lonely sea-strand, a rock marking the resting place of a loved form, and the scent of herbs as the word is spoken that will bridge the world of the living and the dead.

From out of the mist of the west comes the voice of the Celtic Wise Woman, a voice of knowledge that is sometimes heavy with a pain too difficult to carry, sometimes rich in the magic that dwells in rainbow and in crystal spring, sometimes as far away as an echo of long distant horns in the Wild Hunt that screams across the sky before the Horned One, Cernunnos, driving the souls of the dead to the Underworld. And also in our own everyday living, lighting up our own times, revealing the magic around us.

The traditions of Celtic wisdom reach back through centuries, steeped in spells and magic. They are special, no mere system of belief or dogma, but something that can be so integral to daily life – even now – that those who share in them walk in another world, a rich and spiritual land. In many ways this shamanistic culture is similar to the all-embracing way of life of the Native American Indian, so much more real than the materialistic world of the nineties, and bringing concepts like birth and death, meaning and purpose, individual striving, into their rightful place.

Natural magic and richness of living is not some legendary concept that disappeared with the unicorn, with giants and myth. In spirit, if not in physical fact, there have been Celtic Wise Women – called by whatever name – for as long as the Celtic races have existed. I am a follower in highly exalted company, passing on, even at this unlikely moment in time, secrets that were known when the mountains in the mists of the west were fresh and unspoiled.

Yet this is the time when magic is most needed – the ending of the millennium and the coming of the new Age of Aquarius are all prophecy-ridden, promising wonderful beginnings and sinister ends. One can get rather lost in the shaping and moving of celestial events – and it has always been at such times that the confused, feeling they cannot see their way clearly, have felt a need to consult the wise woman or the shaman to get a perspective that will help them to go forward with more confidence. It is at such times, also, that such elusive, shadowy figures emerge from the fabric of legend and mystery to take their place and provide what wisdom and help they are empowered to give. As the proverb goes: 'When the pupil is ready, the teacher will appear'. So when the time is right, the answers are somehow there, for those who ask or look for them.

In the Oak Grove – The Druids

In the popular mind, Celtic beliefs are largely identified with the robed figures of the spiritual leaders who were known as Druids. As a Celtic Wise Woman, I might (it would be reasonable to suppose) describe myself as a

Druidess. But this would not be accurate.

I am not a Druidess. I have never studied the beliefs nor undertaken the training of a Druid, nor felt the need to join the Druidic groups which flourish even today – Druidism having been 'revived' in the eighteenth century. The principles may be the same but much of the tradition and culture of modern Druidism arose from intelligent guesswork (overlaid by a good deal of popular 'Celtic sentimentality') and the evidence of archaeologists. In fact, because of the secrecy of their calling, almost nothing is known of the ancient practices of these mysterious and powerful people except for what Roman historians and commentators chose to record.

They found the Druidic practices – especially human sacrifice – distressingly barbaric, their power troublesome and elusive, and although it was not their policy to persecute the native religious leaders in the areas they conquered – preferring peaceful integration with their own gods – they decided that the hold the Druids seemed to have over the Celtic people challenged their own power. And so in AD 60 they attacked the headquarters of the Druids, the mysterious isle of Anglesey.

The Roman writer Tacitus has recorded how, in blood, smoke and slaughter, the sacred isle was overrun by Roman troops who ransacked it from end to end, desecrating the ceremonial oak groves and overturning the altars. Every person on the island was slaughtered including women, despite the fact that they were terrifying with their long dark robes and tousled hair, carried smoking torches and screamed invective at the invaders.

It was at this same moment in history that the king of the Iceni (a tribe in the south of England) left his kingdom jointly on his death between the Emperor Nero and his two daughters. This was in the hope that the emperor would protect his widow, Boudicca, and the rights of the two girls. But instead, his kingdom was immediately overrun by unscrupulous Roman civil servants and when she protested, Boudicca was treated as a rebel, stripped and flogged. Her daughters suffered multiple rape from the assembled soldiery.

Seething with fury and outrage, Boudicca took upon herself the leadership of the white-hot revolt that had already erupted against the Romans. It gathered momentum with incredible ferocity and barbaric victories. Predictably, it ended in tragedy, slaughter and Boudicca's death, but huge numbers of Roman troops and citizens also died. It is not so much the revolt that is of interest to us, however – it is the fact that Boudicca was, apparently, a Druid, and as such, one of the most famous in history.

She reportedly let loose a hare which she had brought hidden under her cloak, and let it run – some authorities declare, as a signal for the uprising. Others see it as a method of divination regarding the outcome of the battle, while yet other experts, more picturesquely, speak of the hare as a 'totem animal' and mention other religious and magical elements she apparently used.

The Celts – and indeed the Druids – worshipped many gods, and while the rebellion was going on, Roman histories tell that in the sacred oak groves, Druids throughout the country were invoking the terrifying goddess Andrasta, 'the unconquerable'. Boudicca too prayed to her before battle, and the human sacrifice she demanded was paid faithfully and bloodily after each victory.

Who Were the Celts?

The Celtic tradition has sprung, as have all the great beliefs and truths, the great wisdoms of the world, from the nature of the people themselves. So who are, or were the Celts?

Physically, they were a race of people who emerged from the known western world – their origins in the East – in the centuries before Christ. They settled in areas of what is now Europe, but continued to roam extensively – in about 390 BC they sacked Rome, and Celtic bands also penetrated into Greece, where they reverberated through classical history by plundering the Temple at Delphi. They were magnificent and fearless warriors – this, it was declared by military men like Julius Caesar, was because of their belief in the immortality of the soul. They were in fact one of the earliest races to include 'transmigration of souls' and visions of an afterlife in their beliefs – and their phenomenal courage was put down by the Romans to the fact that they thought they would not die but would return again from the world of the dead.

By the time of the Roman invasion of Britain, the Celts were occupying Gaul, Spain, Britain and Ireland. But even the pure Celts who were driven by the invaders to defend their culture in the fastnesses of Scotland, Ireland and Wales, were a difficult people to pin down, their races mixed strains from many different parts of the known western world.

In Britain, they were mainly of three distinct types – the dark stocky descendants of Iberian seafarers who had settled here over 2,000 years before Christ; the Beaker Folk of the Bronze Age who contributed their skills in the arts of working with metal and pottery; and the tall, blond Celts from Gaul, fair-skinned and blue eyed, who fled before the Roman occupation of their land.

When they came, the Celts brought with them the culture, the religion, and the beliefs which characterized their race more than physical type. They established the system which administered these beliefs. It was a deep and personal system, one which involved all members of the community. In the Celtic world, each knew his place – and these were strongly and clearly defined – but, just as important, there was a place for all.

The original beliefs of the Celts were pagan, with a hierarchy of gods and goddesses, based on nature, the world around and the rituals of the changing seasons, the trees, the lakes and streams, ancestor/heroes and tales of their exploits – most of all, the presence of the light and darkness, the sun and the stars. The Druids were indeed the religious leaders of the people, but they were far more than that. Little remains in the way of records, for though the Druids were literate, they did not record their knowledge but passed it on orally. It seems that women as well as men might train to become Druids, and there was no social bar to application, but the training took anything up to twenty years. Druids were politically powerful and their word held such sway that they could depose a king in a few sentences or stop a battle by stepping between the opposing armies.

We normally associate the Celtic tradition with this period of gods and heroes, of the four great religious feasts that made up the Celtic year and were celebrated as the power of the sun grew weaker and then returned in full strength, of the mysteries of the moon. It is overlaid with the qualities of the Celts themselves, intense feeling for nature and awareness of the natural world, richness of thought, imagery, a questioning and a deep spiritual aware-ness. The Celts, at whatever period, did not accept unques-tioningly, they explored other worlds as well as this one if they could, they touched both the extreme heights and the lowest depths. Their feelings contained, often, great beauty, simplicity and they longed in a vague way for inner disci-pline of the soul and spirit.

When the Romans invaded Britain, the Celtic races were forced to retreat before the Roman armies. They fled west-wards, into the fastnesses of the area later to be known as Wales, where they assumed an identity they called the Brotherhood, the 'Cymru'. In the north, the 'Old Welsh' kingdoms of Ystrad Clude (Strathclyde) and Gododdin (Edinburgh) held sway through centuries which produced some of the most magnificent early Welsh poetry, amid the wild Pictish kingdoms of Scotland. The soft mysterious green shores of Ireland were never conquered; there the Celtic tradition found its own rich flowering. Further south, other Celtic tribes had fled into the fastnesses of Cornwall and Brittany, and to the ancient lost kingdoms which traditionally linked them, the most notable being Lyonesse, birthplace of the hero Tristan, whose love story with the Irish princess Isolde forms one of the great romances of the legends of King Arthur.

You do not need to be born in the Celtic lands to find that you have a spiritual affinity with the Celts and their way of life. But the Druids worked – and still do – very much as groups. The Wise Woman works alone, and has always been elusive. No one ever provided training on how to be a Wise Woman. So who is she – and who am I?

A very great deal of the knowledge and wisdom used in this kind of psychic, spiritual work is intuitive, and one has to look for the answers in the same way as the pagan Celts sought for the symbolic messages in their myths and heroic tales. I could only begin with myself in the process of identification as a representative of the ancient Celtic Wise Women who have stood by, in the background, through over twenty centuries, ready to share their awareness of richness and magic, uplift, comfort and counsel, to answer questions of the dark and the light and assist the soul to go forward.

Viewing myself objectively, these are some of the things I see:

Portrait of a Wise Woman

There is no one who can make any claim to be 'qualified' as a Wise Woman. She is chosen, marked from birth. There are no coincidences in psychic and magical work. Spiritually, everything happens for a purpose – though we are given intelligence in order to be able to question and seek the truth for ourselves, rather than to accept blindly.

I am Celtic by birth, born in North Wales into a line (on

my mother's side) of generations of Welsh-speaking native Welshmen and women.

I am left-handed (in long tradition a link with magic and hidden deeds).

My name is Welsh, uncommon outside the Welsh borders. It has both Welsh and French connections (Northern France and Brittany kept something of the Celtic culture): 'delys' from the French *fleur de lys*, the lily that appears on the French royal coat of arms. Traditionally the Welsh meaning of 'Dilys' is 'like the lily' or 'pure as the lily'. This is especially apt when applied to the Wise Woman's endless struggle to hold to the links with the purifying power of the spirit and to free the soul from the darkness and negativity which constantly threaten it.

I did not know for many years, but I was named after a dead baby which sleeps in an all but lost grave in the churchyard of a picturesque Welsh church – my 'family vault' where my Welsh grandparents both also rest. The child was their first-born, and would have been my mother's elder sister, but she died when only a few months old, before my mother's birth. I have a vivid memory of a visit I made on foot, alone in the starry dark of a winter's night to that remote churchyard and the unmarked grave. I had been told to take flowers there, and I did so though no one realized I would have to go there late at night and alone.

I was about twelve, and there were presences around me that night, so I have felt ever after that the little spirit whose name I carry has often been close especially when I am working with the world of the dead – in today's parlance, when I am working as a medium.

But why should the choice of my name be so important? It was arbitrary, you may think, it really means nothing. I might just as well have been named 'Yvonne' or 'Vanessa', which my father wanted.

But when working with magic, one of the first things to be learned is that there is power in a name. It can be used to reveal secrets about you, to perform spells; as personal as your own signature, knowledge of your name leaves you open and vulnerable. It is for this reason that many ancient myths and folk-tales – *Rumpelstiltskin* is an obvious example – concern a contest with the power of evil only overcome if the pure hero or heroine can discover its name. (We will hear more concerning names later.)

It is all too easy to be wise after the event. Though it was not obvious at the time, I can see clearly now that until I was some ten years old, I experienced and displayed constant unmistakable signs that I was an intuitive 'wise child'. After that the manifestations, constantly dismissed as imagination and even naughtiness, were kept to myself and I learned to doubt my own knowledge and experience of reality.

But like small fish appearing one by one at the top of a pond, so that what seemed empty is suddenly teeming with life, the memories, recollections and evidence of that mystic, intuitive past of mine increasingly surface. One example will do: recently I was glancing through a book of rituals and spells. I noticed one detailing how to gather the energy of the five elements by moving within the shape of a pentacle, and remembered how, as a small child (maybe as young as seven) I often sought out grassy spaces, with certain kinds of trees nearby, in the countryside surrounding my home in North Wales. I never knew why, but I would move ceremonially around such spaces, barefoot, in a kind of dance. The book of spells, seen some forty years later, described exactly the movements I used and the places and circumstances which made the ritual more potent. I had intuitively fulfilled every requirement as a child, without having a clue what I was doing. This seemingly amazing coincidence is only one among many which, years later, have proved that I was far wiser than anyone – even myself – suspected. My abilities were choked off by stern dismissal and ridicule, and went underground, as it were, until they resurfaced, strengthened and tested by years of struggle, half a lifetime later.

But perhaps the most convincing evidence I have for my

right to claim the cloak of the Wise Woman is that my birth chart and other relevant divination clearly state that (whether I have been aware of it in the past or not) I possess the Wise Woman's powers and abilities and have done since I was born. A reading was done for me some three years ago by an expert numerologist of Life Maps International. Numerology in this case involved the letters of my name (that all-important name), each of which was given its appropriate number. Their various totals, along with the total of the numbers making up my date of birth, revealed the following characteristics and powers:

Inspirational: Intuitive: Spiritual: Perfection: Second Sight: Clairvoyance: ESP: Universal Power on a physical level: Master Builder for Betterment of others.

From a reading of my birth chart, drawn up by my associate Richard Lawler, it is obvious that similar revelations exist there in the patterns of the stars and planets. Here are some of Richard's comments:

'You were born with a new-age Aquarian moon. This new age is a rediscovery of Celtic/Atlantean magic and spiritual practices as used in the northern tradition of the Odin Yggdrasil Tree of theoretic knowledge, power and wisdom employed in a Druidic co-masonic fashion.

'Your Moon-Trine-Neptune brings you into contact with fairies and people from other realms.

'Mars-Trine-Uranus brings contact with alien thought forms – the *Zeitgeist*/brain/mind/beliefs of aliens. You were born with these abilities.

'Venus in Aries – a willingness to accept sudden encounters and relate them to the history of the past, thus acquiring wisdom.

'Jupiter-Pluto in Leo with the north node of the Moon enables you, through hard work, ritual and ceremony, to project visions into the future in both a personal and political arena.

'Your main geometric pattern of the chart – a rectangle Moon-Neptune-Venus-Pluto – Moon in the twelfth house, gives the ability to travel into such unearthly realms and describe them. This aspect, more than any other, is what you might call a footprint of the gods.'

It is not all easy for a Wise Woman, however. Why does she live alone and avoid people? Often because she is part-unreal and finds it too difficult in the 'real world'. Richard had this accurate comment from my birth chart:

'The Moon here gives an isolated lonely compulsion but cannot avoid contact with the pattern of change in the world.'

In spite of the lack of solid factual evidence, the Wise Woman – that solitary figure which blended, as it were, with the trees, the waters, the quiet places of nature – has actually left her imprint on history, though just as insubstantial as her image are the records and hints that she was indeed a part of Celtic life.

John Murray was the publisher in 1904 of *Gods and Fighting Men: The Story of the Tuatha De Danaan and of the Fianna of Ireland, arranged and put into English by Lady Gregory. With a Preface by W.B. Yeats.* Lady Gregory put into English some of the greatest and most powerful and magical of Celtic myths, tales and folk-poetry which, to those who cannot understand the Gaelic, open up in the translation of the larger-than-life, tapestry-rich, green and blue and gold world of the early Celts. In his preface, Yeats comments that such a world, (filled as it is with heroes and their beautiful, soulful queens) is as though created by children, imagination running riot. 'One remembers,' he says, 'the Druid who answered, when someone asked him who made the world, "The Druids made it".'

Secret Wise Women

From these records, however exaggerated, comes a picture of life as it was in the bright days. And the details are not included in a slap-dash manner. That is why we must sit up and take note when, for perhaps the first time on record, the Celtic Wise Woman steals from the shadows and makes her appearance, in the guise of a 'woman Druid'. For it appears that one of the most marvellous heroes of Irish myth, Finn MacCool, was instructed and educated secretly by such an old woman – in the best tradition of fairy tale, in the depths of the forest.

His father had been killed in battle with his enemies; his beautiful mother was afraid to keep him with her, and so two women, one described as Bodhmall, the woman Druid, arrived to spirit him away to the woods of Slieve Bladhma to nurse him and care for him in secret. As he grew, they instructed him and he became a great warrior.

In the Arthurian tradition, too, the Wise Woman makes her appearance though she does not always use her magical powers unselfishly. The figure of the wizard Merlin who, in a similar manner to the 'woman Druid', educated the young Arthur, is haunted by the figure of his love Nineve, who, having learned enough magic from the great man to ensnare him, traps him for ever in an enchanted wood.

The magical name of the enchantress Morgan le Fay, supposedly the half-sister of Arthur, beckons enticingly through the forests of Arthurian legend and it may be that Nineve and the mysterious Morgan were one and the same.

But aside from the ancient traditions – which are often discovered to be based soundly on historical record – there is the interesting fact that the pagan worshippings of the Celts were vague, varied and confusingly diffuse. If one investigates further, one discovers that it is, after all these centuries, impossible to gain a clear picture of the many-aspected ways in which innumerable gods and goddesses, often of only tribal or local note – though no less powerful – were worshipped in the tangled tracery of their own particular myths. And it is not so much in the formal Druidic tradition that the Wise Woman seems to belong.

Rather she emerges more as a typical pagan 'High Priestess' of the great Earth Mother, the goddess herself who was known throughout history by the names which slid effortlessly into each other from place to place and period to period of historical time: Inanna, Ashtoreth, Isis, Aphrodite, Kwan Yin, Arianrhod, Ishtar, Rhiannon, Erzulie, Freya, Gaia, are just a few of the forms she takes as well, of course, as the Madonna, Mary.

The Goddess and Her High Priestess

In pagan belief, and in the 'old' religions, the High Priestesses were the representatives of the goddess, and during certain ceremonies, were over-shadowed physically by the goddess herself, becoming her physical manifestation. The enchantresses of old – Morgan le Fay, Vivienne, Nineve – even the 'fairy women' who might be described as 'elementals' – the embodiment of magic power which could bewitch and enthrall by means of apparently normal human beauty – might well have been similar aspects of the goddess. As we discover when investigating the subject, nothing is certain.

Wise Woman Today

As a Wise Woman of the 1990s I work alone, and my work, though involving the traditional powers of the psychic: clairvoyance, focused through the tarot; mediumship, contacting the dead; regressions in to past lives, which assist enlightenment and psychological healing, seems to be more and more involved with deep spiritual growth and even with the problems of spirits which are not of this world. I find I am having to stray often into the realms of aliens, space craft, UFOs, the legacy of Atlantis, heavy karmic destinies and how to deal with them, psychic ability

27

and how to deal with it and develop it, even the shamanistic experiences of altered consciousnesses and how to relate them to 'normal' realities. People are referred to me as someone who can help them with problems of 'haunting' and 'possession' that other practitioners do not want to touch. This means that I am never surprised to discover just who I am talking to. I may find myself dealing with an elemental or an alien – neither of whom possess souls as we know them; or a spirit of incredible wisdom and power who actually gives *me* the enlightenment during a sitting; or as on one occasion an unsuspected trance medium who conducted the meeting with me through a deep-voiced and (actually quite bossy) ancient presence or 'other self' whose utterances were of such advanced wisdom that they were hardly comprehensible.

I do tread the magical three worlds of the Celtic visualization, slipping just as easily into the high heavenly planes as the dark lower regions. And I encounter many different 'gods and goddesses' in my work.

Mainly, however, I feel I am a projection – a representative – of the goddess herself. The link was revealed almost as soon as I became aware of my destiny, and I was able to record the messages that were 'channelled' – rather like a silent dictation – into my brain. Being able to communicate mentally, on higher planes, with different intelligences, is a gift which is particularly that of the Wise Woman or shaman. The goddess provided me with a sort of handbook – texts of wisdom, and revealed herself in powerful images that explain, for me, something of what I do and am. It is just as magical as the bright glimpses of the old Celtic world, and I will be including passages for meditation and wisdom – from the goddess and from other sources – throughout the chapters of this book.

I was able to identify the particular goddess who communicates with me as Sirona, a little known Romano-Celtic goddess of healing with shrines in Europe and who is traditionally linked with Apollo (the Roman god of healing). But the Goddess herself is always the same, though she has many faces and many names. To invoke her as a bright and beautiful presence into your life, here is the book's first 'secret', and first 'spell' – an invocation where you may speak to her and also hear her speak in her own voice:

Invocation

Celestial fires which burn incandescent the candles of eternity through the dark of the mysteries of time, of which there was none and is none and yet always will be in the present of the arrested moment, light I charge you the souls which seek me and send the glow-worms of hope and enlightenment to those which humbly wait.

Burning blue upon blue and silver upon silver, descend with the power so that my name may be known throughout the groves and the glades of ancient and everlasting trees. And with flaming candelabrum illuminate the altar in the glade of the goddess so that those who come to worship may lift their eyes and behold my face.

In the texture of the water are my footprints, and in the green leaves is my touch; I walk on the wings of the morning and the silk robe of the night showers me with stars.

For the maiden is the crown of the mysteries studded with round stones that are my gems; from the sacred chalice spills the wine of ecstasy, and across the great arch of the sky the starry bodies meet in passionate joy.

I am, I was and I will always be. Still in the shadows, waiting. At my feet are the votive garlands put there by ancient worship-pers and from the withered blossoms arises the perfume of jasmin and sandalwood, of the night-blooming starry flowers which are silver and yet are vibrant scarlet, studded with dewdrops of living blood from the dark and the light worlds when the moon is down.

Make me your offering and veil your eyes in my presence if you would know me, for I am awful and beautiful and only the trem-

bling heart which acknowledges the power within me may know also my generosity and my protection.

2

Love Spells and Other Love Secrets

'I have a pen-friend arriving to stay for the weekend,' confided the eager voice of the enquirer at the other end of the phone. It was an attractive, mature voice, and I judged her age as mid-fifties or so. 'Can you tell me if he will be the one for me?'

I laid out the relevant tarot cards and told her what I had found, as tactfully as I could.

'The central card is very sexual,' I admitted. 'It doesn't necessarily mean you have found true love though. As a matter of fact, it generally indicates some sort of sexual difficulty, sexual pain – or even an inclination towards violent sex. You – um-' I cleared my throat '—are not a virgin, are you?' (I was aware that she had never been married.)

'Oh, no,' she said blithely. 'But I expect he will want to jump straight into bed, like all the rest. Men are all the same, aren't they?'

'Well, what do you think about that?' I queried.

'I can't wait,' she said, with relish.

Feeling rather like a Victorian nanny, I advised her to take all possible precautions, and not rush into anything – which the cards indicated she was temperamentally prone to doing. I felt personally that her expectations were such that no mere male would have been able to live up to them.

'But if this is what you want, go ahead and enjoy your-self,' I finished. A person in her mid-50s has a right to decide for herself what her morals are. As an afterthought, I asked: 'What is your actual age, by the way?'

'Eighty-one,' she trilled crisply.

There is no limit of age or anything else on the hope of love or the expectation that, if achieved, it will bring the recipi-ent their heart's desire. And throughout the ages, there have been two main preoccupations which have driven men – or more particularly women – to consult the Wise Woman. They have risked name, position, the fear of God and of their husbands and fathers, for the magical potion to attract love to themselves. And, as a counter-balance, the poison to deal with rivals who might be in their way.

I have many times been approached, particularly by women of Eastern extraction – more than Western women, they are at home with the idea of spells and magic – who plead nakedly for 'something that will bring him back' or 'something that will make him love me again'. Though I could provide such secret formulae I tell them that I do not deal in that kind of instant miracle as a rule, but that I will discuss their problem with them and try to help them see why their man lost interest in the first place, and what they can do to help themselves using less drastic methods.

The result, whether as the result of a spell or ritual, or an intelligent, commonsensical psychological understanding of the situation, will probably be the same in the end – the important factors in the situation being the willingness of the seeker to change things and the effort and positive energy she (or he) has put into it. But there are some temperaments and mentalities that do not want to try and understand the workings of their 'miracles' and their 'magic'.

In the bazaars of the East, no doubt the transaction would take only a few seconds as the love-potion and the fee changed hands. There are practitioners in the West who offer such philtres or their equivalent, and who, in London at least, can charge anything up to a thousand pounds for their services.

When one bears in mind that the 'love' so earnestly sought by those who come for sittings and consultations is often mainly concerned with sexual attraction and power, the 'love potion' does make some sense, for there are of course plenty of substances and objects which have proven aphrodisiac properties. And I can advise women on what their men are thinking and feeling, what they are finding attractive in someone else, and how the situation can best be dealt with so that they can bring the straying ram back into the fold, as it were. But this has to be essentially a long-term thing.

A night of mad passion can be easily conjured up, but it is what is going to happen the next morning that bothers me. A relationship is not concerned only with mad passion, and while an understanding of their situation will be beneficial for the rest of their lives for women 'wanting him to love me again', the purchase of a 'love-potion' guaranteeing that night of passion does not bring with it also a user's manual or covering insurance if something should go wrong once the passion has burned itself out.

Magic and Spells

What the average person does not understand about magic is that, in the first place, you get exactly what you ask for, and only that. Secondly, you must pay in some way for what you get. Fairy tales and old myths, all the lore of folk wisdom, are full of accounts of the tricky nature of wishes and spells and how magic can backfire. King Midas, for instance, was granted his wish for everything he touched to be turned to gold – and at first he was enchanted by his fortune as it blossomed under his hand.

But in the end, he found to his horror that he could not eat golden bread, nor drink golden water.

A friend who is a powerful psychic recently recounted to me the tale of Gilda, whose lover had left her, and who was in despair, thinking she had lost him. She mixed the love-potion she obtained on consulting a self-confessed 'witch' with all the relevant ingredients – including a few drops of her own menstrual blood, which is extremely magical because of its feminine links with the power of the moon (and thus the goddess). Gilda managed to get the mixture into her lover's cup of coffee and he drank it.

This kind of toxic cocktail, often including items like Shakespeare's 'eye of newt and toe of frog', as well as the infallible drops of menstrual blood, has long been used in desperate cases, for its sheer power. The relics of childbirth – the caul from the face of the child, the placenta and so on – were equally powerful when used in magic, for the mysteries of the feminine, linked to the goddess through the moon, have always been stronger and deadlier than those of the sun – which is her masculine counterpart. Interestingly, Shakespeare must have been aware of this, and his witches' brew also included:

'Finger of birth-strangled babe,
Ditch-deliver'd by a drab.'

Gilda's love-spell, fortunately, was not so drastic. But did it work?

'He came back five times in one day for sex,' my friend reported. 'And they were married within a few months. But she never had children, even after years of treatment – and she had been desperate to marry just so she could have a child. And as well as that, he brought his mother to live with them, and Gilda's married home life was ruined. So although her wish seemed to come true, she lost out on the things she really wanted.'

Complicated results which grant the wish but actually make things worse are one reason why magic should not be handled except by someone who knows what they are doing, and this is particularly true when dealing with affairs of the heart. The repercussions can be very unexpected and painful, and it is in our loves, romances and passions that we are at our most vulnerable.

In cases of this sort, I try to establish the true state of things by means of clairvoyance, which, more than anything else, can reveal to me exactly what the sitter really thinks and feels, and also what their partner's true feelings are. Many times it becomes obvious that though the person concerned is not happy, and perhaps the partner is just as miserable, there is some sort of traumatic bond which will hold them together in a permanent 'no-win' situation. They will not be able to part, so anything that helps to lighten the load, as it were, is a bonus. A spell or some magic, in this situation, can make a real difference, even though it may only be temporary.

But if a situation has broken down altogether, if a relationship has outgrown itself in a more drastic manner and either or both of the partners have nothing binding them except negative responses like resentment, indifference, or possibly even pity, I do not consider that nights of passion are the answer. In their right time, all things must pass and it is not the place of the Wise Woman or magician to meddle with this type of change.

Natasha, aged nineteen, was in the throes of having been jilted by her boy friend. She was intense, passionate and had been deeply infatuated. It was not possible for me to tell her that what she had felt had not been love in the truest sense, that her pain would pass and that in time, the man she worshipped now would become just a small blip on her emotional screen.

'I can't live without him,' she sobbed. 'Please, please, get him back for me.'

Her suffering was terrible and very genuine. She had been deeply disillusioned by life for the first time, and acutely wounded. But an instant cure, happiness on demand, is not what my work is about. I knew that Tasha would recover from her suffering, and that the pain was part of her spiritual path. Spells which block the progress of the soul, rub out the lessons the personality has been set, magically restore Romeo and Juliet radiance to couples whose greed and selfishness have made their relationship into a bitter battlefield, are not the concern of the Wise Woman. Wisdom – in love as everywhere else – does not come from ducking blows that fate hands out, failing to face up and to take responsibility when things go wrong or do not work out as we would like.

Real and True Love

I have already mentioned my ability to link in to, and record, ancient wisdom. It is like being able to read and record the words written on the wind or in the rippling of the waters. They are often inspirational and symbolic, for images and symbols are far more usual than words when communicating with the spirit and the soul. Here is a meditation on real and true love:

Meditation

Many speak of love and tread the path to find it. We do not speak of it nor try to find it for it is an illusion. We have passed the many-faceted rainbow bridge and gone beyond the sunset and the dawn.

As the moon is light and darkness, so we are to each other. As the void is filled with nothing so we are to each other. As the sea is full of water and the waterfall of sound so we are to each other. As joy is joyful and laughter is full of delight so we are to each other.

In order to achieve complete union with another it is necessary to detach yourself from them. Only when you have cut yourself off completely will you find yourself within the embrace for which you yearn. Only when you have renounced desire will you achieve the longing of your heart.

There can be no loss, no loneliness, if you have never taken possession but have only borrowed, delighting in the gift, and returned it in humility and gratitude.

It is very difficult for the average person to conduct their love affair on that sort of elevated level. And as a Wise Woman, I am more aware than most that in spite of the fact that nineties woman (and nineties man) is popularly supposed to be psychologically and sexually adept, freed from the nasty little misconceptions and blind spots which plagued earlier generations, able to take or leave affairs (of whatever sort) and capable of finding complete fulfilment on every level with no trouble at all, this is not in fact the case. There is a deep and desperate need for love, for romance, for an ability to communicate, for understanding about why the whole business is, still, so difficult and confusing.

This practical level is where we move next. For without necessarily interfering with the progress of the soul, there is a great deal that can be done to help those who yearn to achieve the love that they so anxiously crave. Love does not always bring with it bliss and happiness, but it is by experiencing the pain as well as the joy of loving that life is enriched and the learning process along the spiritual path proceeds.

So here it is – your book of secrets for successful love. You will have come across some of them before, for they are based – as all magic is – on simplicity and common sense. Wisdom is never complicated. If it is, there is something wrong. Ancient cures, spells and rituals have been passed down over centuries, being sometimes in the popular fashion, sometimes forgotten. Not all the notes in this Love Book will appeal to you, and that is as it should be, for everyone is different. Choose those that seem to speak to you personally, and do not try any that make you feel uncomfortable or silly. Good luck and may you find happiness in your loving.

Your Love Book

Uncertain, tense, painfully diffident and insecure people rarely attract anyone. Mostly, they do not feel they deserve to be loved, even though they desperately want to be. They feel hideously unworthy and embarrassed if someone pays them a compliment. Or they may suspect some ulterior motive behind an appreciative manner or invitation.

Recognize yourself? In that case, before attempting the spell for attracting a lover, you need to spend some time learning how to love yourself, and to feel you are worthy of the wonderful relationship which is waiting somewhere for you, if only you have the confidence to believe in it.

Loving Yourself

In order to start feeling good about yourself, carry out the following straight away:

1. Choose a rose quartz gemstone at a New Age or similar establishment. All quartz crystals embody power and magic. The rose quartz is a lovely soft pink in colour, and contains properties of self love and self confidence. Take time over this, and be sure you feel a personal link with your stone. This is why it is better to choose one for yourself rather than ask someone else to buy it for you, or even let the vendor pick one out. I usually advise sitters to choose one they can wear round their neck, in a rough unpolished state, for the hardness of the gem will be felt against the skin, and it is easily to hand if at times of doubt and insecurity – during the dark hours of the night, for instance – you feel in need of some reassuring talisman to touch or hold.

When you acquire any gem, wash it in clear water (preferably running, or salt). This clears it of all the other energies it might have picked up before you obtained it. Then consciously dedicate it to yourself, speaking aloud words you feel at ease with. Perhaps something along the lines of:

I am (your name – e.g. Mary Smith), and I choose you as my
stone, to work with me from this moment and help me to achieve
the ability to love myself and the confidence to believe in myself,
to believe that I am worthy of real, true and unselfish love and that
I will be able to respond to it with dignity, with warmth and with
mutual passion and delight.

Thank your stone for allowing you to choose it and for the help it will give you. There are spirits in all natural things, and they often provide us with support, assistance and encouragement while we are literally trampling them (as in the case, say, of grass or sea-sand) underfoot. By becoming aware of what is actually present physically around you, you will become aware also of allies whose purpose is always to comfort and wish you well.

There may be some readers who, by this time, are thoroughly embarrassed at the idea of addressing a gemstone or thanking the grass for providing coolness and balm to those who walk on it. I am afraid they will probably never even become novices with regard to magic. There are some people like that – but I hope you do not feel so restricted.

It is generally necessary (for obvious reasons) to carry out rituals and your own special spells in private. If at first you do feel rather silly and inhibited, do not worry. When learning any new skill or craft, there is a period of clumsiness and awkwardness. Concentrate more on the results and the ways in which you relax into this new world, rather than the seemingly strange methods you need to employ in order to communicate with it.

2. Your second ritual – much mentioned in self-help manuals – to assist you to love yourself and feel you can accept the idea of love from others from a position of equality, is what I call the Mirror Spell.

Always be honest with yourself when dealing with magic and spells, when diagnosing your failings and identifying exactly what your wishes really are. Most people delude themselves. You need not admit any of these private thoughts to others, but it is vital that you are aware in your own mind of exactly what your aims are and where you want to go – or, often, *not* go.

With regard to love, sex or affairs, this sort of personal honesty can mean all the difference between happiness and peace of mind, or a pattern of disaster that repeats itself over and over. If you do not feel you are loveable, then you will be unable to cope with true love if it is offered to you, or you will despise anyone who shows signs of loving you, privately feeling that if they can accept and be satisfied with *you*, there must be something wrong with them.

There are many people who, far from being unable to appreciate photos of themselves, do not even feel comfortable when they look at their reflection in a mirror. In fact, this is not as silly as it sounds for, as we have already seen with names, images or representations of the self are extremely charged with magic. Accounts of primitive tribes who are frightened by cameras or terrified if they see their reflection in a glass are not just examples of unsophisticated, rather naïve behaviour in people who have not been educated to know better. In many religions and ancient cults, both the reflection and also the name – the *real* name, often kept deadly secret while a nickname or everyday name was used – was considered as much a vital, intimate part of each individual as his own body.

It is sometimes thought that the name, reflection or photograph contains the soul, and as such, images and names are intensely vulnerable. Injury or even death can be inflicted if others are allowed this personal, intimate knowledge.

I can remember that even as a child, long before I was aware of any destiny as a Wise Woman, I had an inexplicable reluctance to reveal my name to anyone, even school-teachers. I used pseudonyms in my writing (at twelve years old) and when I went on holiday during my teens, I informed new acquaintances (inaccurately) that my 'real' name was not really my name at all. Letters used to arrive addressed to people my family had never heard of.

Matters reached a head when, while newly employed as a barmaid in my early twenties, I was asked by several of the regulars in the bar what my name was. I still did not know why, but I would not tell them. I refused to answer.

'Come on, you must have a name,' they said, and, desperately, I replied that it was – um – (joke!) Esmeralda. Suspicious enquiries from my boss – who knew the real name under which I had applied for the job, and who asked bluntly: 'Well what on earth *are* you called?' resulted in my being addressed, throughout the time of my employment by the compromise 'Esme'. I still managed to avoid letting my real name become public property.

One of the first things lovers do at the beginning of a relationship is to 'rechristen' each other with pet names to be used only between themselves. And nearly all lovers carry with them an image of their beloved. Both these habits are illustrative of natural magic – to recreate and to be able to protect your loved one at all times.

The Mirror Spell
This may be used in various ways. If you are aware, however privately, that you do not rate yourself very highly, and don't like to look at your reflection because it makes you feel embarrassed or displeased, begin in the following way:

i. Make sure you are alone with your mirror, and not likely to be interrupted. A hand mirror will do at this stage.

ii. Look directly and clearly at your reflection, straight into the eyes.

iii. Train yourself to be aware that you are looking beyond the image to your Self, your Soul, the hidden and vulnerable part of you that psychiatrists call the 'inner child'. Speak to this hidden self fearlessly.

iv. Since your main objective is to cultivate a sense of self-worth and self-respect and an awareness that you are worthy of love, address your 'inner child' by name and reassure it that you love it. Suitable phrases to use are:

Hello, Mary (or whatever your name is) I am so glad to see you. I love you, you know. Don't worry any more, because now that I am here, we will help each other. Everything will be all right now. I will take care of you, and look after you.

As a variation, look your reflection straight in the eyes and tell him/her how good-looking/beautiful they are, and how proud you are of them.

Hello Mary/Joe, did you know you have stunningly attractive eyes? They are my favourite colour, the most gorgeous blue/grey/brown. And did you know you have lovely skin/wonderful bone structure/an irresistible mouth?

Try to find one genuinely admirable feature to start with – everyone has at least one, even if it is their excellent teeth or well-shaped hairline. Once you have started to concentrate on the things you can feel positive about and approve of, you will find that after only a relatively short period of time, your reflection will take on a life of its own, and will greet you one day with an involuntary smile and tell *you* how gorgeous you are, and how it loves *you*.

The face and bearing of someone who has been told that morning that he or she is loved and can accept this, even if it is your own reflection that is your lover, changes from shyness, diffidence and uncertainty to glowing confidence. And it is a fact of love that a person who looks as though they have one lover immediately draws the attention of others. Do not kid yourself that someone will be attracted to you because you are free and available. Love attracts love, and when you are conducting a love affair with yourself – though not in a selfish, narcissistic fashion – you will find that others want to get in on the act. The glow of loving – even though only yourself – will illuminate your face, your body and the way you move, your whole attitude.

3. Use your space. You need lots of room for this. Stand

in the middle of a large, empty space – a gym for instance, or even out of doors in a field or a big garden. Feel your feet firmly rooted to the ground (in psychic terms, this sense of being connected with terra firma is called 'earthing' or 'grounding'). Now reach up with your hands, and bring them down on each side of your body until you are stretching your fingers right out wide on a level with your shoulders. Imagine that, apart from your physical body, you are carrying other, invisible bodies with you, like a set of Russian dolls, each held within another. These are your etheric, your astral and other spirit bodies – up to as many as twelve of them. As you reach out on each side, imagine your arms are reaching out for some thirty feet, all of which is taken up with you and your bodies.

Have you ever said impatiently that 'I must have my space' or complained that people are 'crowding you out'? It is this sort of space that you mean when you feel you are being pushed into a corner, or made to feel intrusive or too big, awkward and ungainly.

In order to achieve the poise which comes from feeling happy with yourself, your size and the way you are, reach out every day and feel the space around you, then take that space with you everywhere you go – perhaps not thirty feet, but the comfortable six feet or so where your aura can rest without being squashed or made to feel that it is in the way. In lifts, or on crowded streets, a person who can stand or sit quietly, giving the impression that they are not being jostled or intimidated, draws the attention of others, who are fascinated because *they* feel only too put upon. Achieve personal harmony and balance within yourself, and others will be drawn to share it – and be drawn to feel they need you in their lives and cannot manage without you.

Love Spells
We have seen that selfishness in magic and spells will in the end work against the person who casts the spell. Examine your motives carefully before you undertake any of these

love-spells. They will work for you – but in some way you will have to pay for what you obtain. It is also inherent in magic that negative forces (like selfishness or spite) will, in the end, return to the place of their origin and wreak negative havoc on their originator. As a working rule, remember that if you give out love and positivity, that is what you will receive. If you give out negativity, this is what you will find coming back to you.

Love Spell For a Man

To Attract the Woman of his Choice

A man wishing to attract a woman to him should gather together seven blue beads (preferably turquoise-coloured) and a length of thin golden thread.

Begin the ritual at moonrise on Friday (the day connected with the goddess).

First pronounce the following words: *I am* (your name) *You are* (the name of the woman you want or some identifying phrase like 'The woman in red with the long blonde hair') *And with this thread I will bind you to me.*

Carefully knot one end of the thread, so that the beads will stay on it, then slip each bead on one by one, tying a knot in between. As you do so, repeat the following:

With this knot I tie your heart to mine in hope, strength and the power of love.

Repeat seven times until all the beads are on the thread. Then tie the ends of the thread together to make a circlet and repeat:

As this circle we are bound. No beginning and no end. No longer free. I to you and you to me.

Hang the thread near an open window so that it may draw the woman you want to you.

Love Spell For a Woman

To Attract the Man of Her Choice

To cause the man she desires to come to her, the woman should, over the period from the New Moon until the Full

44

Moon, gather every day a feather which should ideally be that of an eagle or wild bird of prey. (However, since they are symbolic, any kind of bird feathers will do if reasonably large, even chicken, or pet budgie!) Place the feather you gather each night together with the others in your room, near your bed.

On the night of the Full Moon, go out of doors at midnight. Take the feathers in your left hand, hold them in a bunch and bind them roughly together with thin string or cotton wound around them, repeating the words:

I am (your name, e.g. Mary Jones), *You are* (his name if you know it, otherwise an identifying phrase such as 'The man in the coffee shop/library/train with dark hair and blue eyes'). *I have watched you as the wild bird flying free, and with this cord I check your flight and hold your wings and draw you down to me.*

Place on the ground before you a scattering of caraway seeds and a fragment of meat and repeat:

The lure, the meat, to bring you to my feet and into my heart. Come soon and we will not part.

Lay the bunch of feathers down with the meat and caraway seeds (which protect against partings). After a few moments, carry the feathers back indoors with you and lay them, bound, near your mirror or a picture of yourself and wait for the man you want to come to you.

Love Spell
To Break With a Lover

If you want to leave a husband/wife/lover and are finding it difficult and painful, the following will ease the emotional strain.

Imagine the sexually charged link that has been forged over the period of time you have been together, remembering that sexual magic is extremely potent. Visualize it as a thick golden rope reaching from your solar plexus to that of your partner. The solar plexus is approximately just above the navel. Visualize the link holding you together so that however far apart you may be, the rope will reach, and pull you towards each other.

To break away, you must sever the link.

Immerse your body in water, and with your left hand make a cutting motion, scissors-like, opening and closing your fingers. Cut through the golden rope that is reaching out from you, with the fingers of your left hand, and imagine the cut ends drifting away from each other. Repeat the following as you think of the person you want to leave: *I cut the link that binds me to you, and I let you go in love and peace. I sever the ties that bind us and I am once again my own free spirit, and owe you no allegiance. There is nothing to hold us and I leave you free and free myself. Fare well, and fare well and fare well.*

Love Gifts

Tokens exchanged have meaning and significance. Follow the language of the flowers, and achieve love or heighten interest by presenting any on this list to the girl or man you love (or want to love):

Wreath or spray of apple blossom I prefer you
Bluebells . . . . .I will be patient and true
White rosebud . . . . .I have an unawakened
                               heart
Roses . . . . .Love, *love*, LOVE
Yellow rose . . . . .I am a jealous lover
White rose . . . . .Yes, I am worthy of
                               your love
Red and white roses together . . . .In spite of the common
    belief that red and white flowers together are unlucky, red and white roses signify strength and unity – double the luck, double the love
Carnations, red . . . . .There goes my heart
         striped . . . . .The answer is – no, no
                             no – oh, well, you win
           pink . . . . .I speak for a woman in
                             love

Chrysanthemum, red . . . . .All my love, all my
kisses

Forget-me-not . . . . .True to you

The Language of Magic

i

This is the first of the 'Magical Dictionaries' I will be including to elaborate and comment on some of the words, terms and psychic or magical details mentioned in the preceding pages. I will clarify references which may not be familiar to readers and make any comments which are of interest but do not fall within the scope of the chapter where the reference appeared.

Age of Aquarius This is an astrological term, and Aquarius is the eleventh sign of the zodiac (Pisces being the twelfth or final one). According to the calculations of astrologers, reaching back thousands of years, we pass through the age of each sign in turn, each age lasting for two thousand one hundred and fifty years. In order to complicate matters even more, the ages have, in this connection, been proceeding in reverse, so that we are at present at the end of the Piscean Age, and entering the Age of Aquarius, which will carry us (if the Earth still exists by then) on to 4000 AD and beyond.

Alien The term alien is commonly used to describe any being or entity which is not of the earth as we know it, and which has its origin in some other planet. Popularly, there is only one sort of alien, which can, however, alter its appearance, or assume a human likeness.

In fact, when one begins to investigate aliens and study recorded encounters with them, as well as open communications – which I have done in my role as Wise Woman – it becomes obvious that aliens exist on many planes, not just the physical plane we are aware of daily. There are two types which commonly appear in records of encounters – one sort are very tall and thin, of a silvery-skinned, hairless appearance; the other sort are much shorter, perhaps three feet high, similarly silvery and hairless, but more aggressive.

When working on the various mental planes, I have found that there are endless other groups (or whatever word seems appropriate) of alien beings. The main thing which characterizes them all is that they are literally alien to us. They are usually frighteningly cold in every sense. However, in the contacts I have made with them, I have discovered that none of them seems likely to invade the Earth or behave in the ways in which they are portrayed in films. Mostly, they are not very interested in the Earth or the human race. Neither, though, are they likely to become touchingly attached to helpful children or anyone else who extends a friendly hand. These are human concepts, and aliens possess no human characteristics at all. They give me the impression that they are simply other races, other groups, very different from human beings but, in their own ways, wrapped up in the working out of their own destinies, just as humanity is on the Earth plane.

Aura Everything that exists is made up from energies that vibrate, and the aura is the envelope of energy which encloses a human body, in which colours can sometimes be seen. I occasionally 'see' colours in the aura clairvoyantly, but my work with it mostly involves healing, touching and smoothing the aura at about three inches away from the body. Often the energies in the aura are tangled or snagged, and at times the spirit of a powerful healer I have come to know as the Eskimo doctor is able to take over my hands and work through me, repairing the aura so that the wounds to the body which have penetrated through it will heal.

Divination   The practice of foretelling the future.

Elemental   Creatures born of the elements, earth, air, fire and water. Types of fairies created from natural energy, usually close to nature. Water and tree sprites are called naiads and dryads. Elementals are usually childlike and often mischievous. They lack deep feelings and, while possessing fairy beauty, will almost certainly be amoral.

Grounding   Psychic abilities and training enable the spirit to leave the earthly body at will and visit higher spiritual planes. Few people who are able to do this return enthusiastically to their human condition, for compared with the spirit the human state is restricted, heavy, clumsy. But since we are all human beings and have accepted our human state as necessary at this time in our development, we do return. We must return fully so that the balance between the physical and the spiritual is as it should be.

Many people find that at times they are not making the necessary contact with the earth – they lose the sense of being 'grounded' – and their spirit may seem to be flying helplessly, as it were, unable to settle into physical reality. This does not need to be something of which one is psychically aware, and can have many ramifications. My own experience over many years is that the mental states identified as hyperactive or even manic may be connected to a lack of 'grounding'.

In any situation which causes an apparent loss of control, of agitation and feeling 'unreal', you can ground yourself by wearing the appropriate gem stone round your neck, or keeping it near at hand. Black haematite or black onyx work effectively, but once you feel you are 'grounded' or if you are experiencing heaviness and a sense of oppression, stop wearing the stone and you will immediately feel your energy lighten.

Ground yourself also by walking on grass, imagining your feet are part of the ground, and that each step is difficult, that there are roots pulling you down. Hold the trunk of a tree and feel it support and steady you in physical reality. Be aware of the air and learn to breathe correctly. Feel yourself take on shape and substance, and be content just to *be*.

Karma The law of cause-and-effect under which we must settle our debts from the past, and according to which we are creating our futures by our actions in the present.

Pentacle A five-pointed, star-shaped image containing many triangles, signifying 'intervention'. Often worn or used by occultists in the past, it has popularly acquired a slightly sinister meaning. In fact, if it is worn with a single point upwards, it signifies 'protection' in the same way as any other protective symbol; it is only if worn with two points upwards and one at the bottom (upside down, as it were) that there is any connection with the dark forces of magick.

Shaman Another name for a medicine-man or woman, someone who is able to enter other planes through altered states of consciousness, to control the powers of spiritual force and communicate with the divine being.

Spell Combination of words and actions which, if performed correctly in accordance with established instructions, will effect a desired result. A ritual is similar, but while a spell is a 'one off', and its effect is not repeated – things have changed or been caused to happen – rituals are performed regularly to keep the *status quo* favourably balanced.

Totem Totem animals, birds or plants were identified in Celtic thought with different gods, goddesses, types of force or natural energy. The whole formed a representative picture of the living world, the seen and the unseen, an incredibly complex web that led by magic and mystery to the centre point of existence, the divine.

In a later chapter, you will be instructed on how to find your own special totem animal, whether cat, snake or whatever, and how to benefit from its powerful protection and support in your life.

Wicca The system of belief and worship known popularly as witchcraft. The old English words 'wic' or 'witch' actually meant nothing more than clever or wise.

3

Dark World Beyond the Grave

Is it the wind sighing, the water murmuring,
Or a voice, passionate with longing, that whispers down
    the centuries 'Guinevere-?'
Does the sun flash blindingly only through the trees
Or on hair that falls like a cascade of gold
Across his arms as he holds her?

I am cold suddenly, in spite of the sun's warmth
As though foreknowledge struck chill to the bone.
The mist has nearly all vanished
And with it has gone the enchantment.

> Welsh Tapestry (Yvaine Huath)

The Death card in the Tarot pack signifies changes, letting
go, a new beginning, a fresh start, a wonderful emergence
from the chrysalis. There is no absolute death, only a different sort of life. We each choose whether we will make it
positive or negative for Death itself is neither good nor bad,
it is just one more fact of living.

> Yvaine Huath

Next, perhaps to love, the human mind is most fascinated
with death in all its forms, from a morbid fear of its own
death and speculation on what will come after, to a concern
with loved ones who have already passed on, a nostalgic
longing for times that will never return, a desire to follow
and communicate just once more with mothers, fathers,
husbands, wives, children.

As a medium, I have come across all kinds of attitudes in
the living towards their dead. At a psychic fair held in a

nightclub, I listened while Mary, a straightforward middle-aged blonde woman asked me to contact her mother. I did so, and when we had identified the spirit which revealed itself, I told Mary to speak to it and that it would hear her.

With no embarrassment, she began:

'Hello, Mum, it's me again. I just want to fill you in on what has been happening since the last time I spoke to you. We're all very well, though Gran's chest is playing up a bit, and Jake fell off his bike and scraped his knee quite badly, and even Tibby has got some infection that is making her fur fall out, but the vet gave us some medication that seems to be working.

'The garden is lovely just now, the daffs and narcissus and tulips are all out, and we've had the drive in front of the garage done with tarmac. Dad comes over every Sunday, as always, and when the weather gets warmer, we're going to start having a barbecue on the patio.

'Jenny's going camping in France with her school soon, and Doug and I were thinking of Egypt this year – a bit of a splash-out with the money, but if we go in the summer when it's very hot there, we might be able to get something at a price we can afford . . . .'

For a full twenty minutes, Mary spoke as unaffectedly as if her mother was sitting there making up a physical three-some with us. I did not contribute a single word (though I continued to 'hold' the spirit of her mother in my mind). She chatted on without stopping, filling in all the little family details, and then finished abruptly:

'Well, I think that's all, Mum. Just to let you know we're all right – and I know you are, and I'll be in touch again soon. Bye bye for now, Mum, lots of love from all of us.'

She might have been dictating a letter. And after 'signing off' she turned and looked at me for the first time.

'Thank you very much. I feel so much better now.'

After I had mentally returned the spirit of her mother to the realms where it belonged, Mary rose and went briskly on her way. To her, a reassuring twenty minutes with her departed Mum was as normal a part of everyday life as ordering an extra pinta from the milkman. Her love and trust, in its unsophisticated innocence, had the power to turn the frowning gates and locks between life and death into a path through a sunny garden. But in some cases, it is the extremes of shock and tragedy which drive those who might not normally take such action to consult a medium.

Norma and Irene, two sisters, came together to see me. Their brother had recently, shockingly, committed suicide, but as if that was not enough, the family had been stunned when, immediately afterwards, a complete stranger appeared at their home declaring that he had been the young man's homosexual lover, and that according to a letter in his possession, the dead boy had left him every single thing he owned.

'We wouldn't mind if we were really sure it was what Bernard wanted,' Irene said quietly, with incredible self-restraint. 'But there are several thousands of pounds in his building society account, and his car – and Mum isn't well, and she and Dad are his next of kin, they are entitled to at least half – she could have a holiday. But she insists that because of the letter – and it is obviously his own hand-writing, not faked – this dreadful man must have it all, every penny.'

'We had no idea he was gay. There is only this man's word for it, and we have no proof at all. None of us has ever heard Bernard so much as mention him,' Norma added. 'We think he must have driven Bernard to take his life somehow, made him write the letter or something, threat-ened him. It is all so terrible – we don't know why he did it, we have no idea. Do you think you could contact him? Ask him whether it is what he really wants? We're sure he would not have wanted Mum to have nothing . . . .'

Solange handed me a sheaf of documents as soon as she had sat down. She had a continental chic that gave her expensive beauty and designer elegance its own individual perfection. Dark glossy hair, sapphire eyes – surely one might have thought, catching the faintest breath of the perfume that seemed to sum up her whole presence – surely this woman could have no black worries. Yet I knew this was one case when appearances could not have been more deceptive.

'Here is a photograph of Julie, and a picture of the hostel where she was found,' she said, her husky French voice as steady as though we were conducting a business transaction. 'This letter is in her handwriting, and her diary. And if you wish something that she possessed, this is her crucifix, she had it when she was eighteen on her birthday. Will that be enough?'

I assured her it was more than enough. The purpose of her visit was to try and contact the spirit of her 19-year-old daughter, who had, while making a walking tour alone in the French countryside, been found dead in a remote hostel.

'Drugged, the police said, but—' Solange shrugged helplessly – 'she had never taken drugs – and would she inject herself with morphine, a huge overdose, in a strange place, with no word to anybody – and on her way home to take up her studies at the university? She was like life itself, full of light. It is impossible, impossible.'

I held the objects she had brought, then her hands, to make the link.

'I will see whether we can find out what did happen to her. And, if she did not do it herself, who was the person responsible for her murder – if it was murder.'

Speaking to the Dead

Most of the people who consult a medium in order to contact the dead have a specific reason for doing so. It is rarely out of idle curiosity and they are often nervous or even a little frightened. Outweighing their fears, however, is their greater need – of enlightenment, of comfort and reassurance in bereavement; or the desire just to say 'I love you' or 'goodbye'. To those who are left behind, the finality of death can often seem like 'unfinished business' which will be settled only after the necessary rituals have been carried out.

There is sound psychology in the ancient ways of physically parting with the dead, of laying out the body for all to see, of tearing one's hair, beating one's breast, screaming and bewailing one's grief. Unexpressed grief can 'kill' the person who has been bereaved from within in a kind of sympathetic dying and although the barriers between the living and the dead can easily be breached, they are between the physical and the spiritual planes. On a purely physical level, death is horrifyingly final, and the physical body can never return.

If you wish to communicate with a loved one who has died, very simple magic will do it for you without the intervention of a medium. All you need is love and trust – but in most cases the huge barrier of doubt, thrown up by the rationality of the brain, gets in the way. Real magic is something apart from rational thinking or logic and in order to achieve it, you need to put the mumblings of your brain on one side.

Most people would be satisfied simply to feel they had made real contact with a loved one, particularly if they want to give the departed person a message themselves. Mostly, enquirers are sensible enough to realize that long chats over the garden wall, as it were, are not very likely to materialize. Sometimes they may want reassurance in their weakness and loneliness, but most do not actually expect or need long or detailed conversation from the other side. The main human requirement is to be reassured that the departed spirit is still there in some shape or form, and that it is all right.

The great anxiety to tell loved ones 'I love you' and 'I miss you' is actually so that the bereaved person will feel better. Souls which have crossed the barrier into the spirit do not need to be told such things, they are aware of them without reassurance, and I personally have found in my work as a medium that spirits which, freed from the physical body, can communicate on the higher planes by telepathic means, are rather surprised when told 'I love you, I miss you'. They are already fully aware of these lovely feelings, and have sent their own reassurances back before the person communicating them actually says a word.

But it brings peace of mind and balm to the soul if the bereaved – or those who still miss loved ones after quite long periods of time – can feel they have made contact and put their message of love across. Many people actually find their own way to the magic – as with all magic, it is simple and obvious to the soul that believes in trust and faith.

Preparation

A photograph of the person you want to contact is ideal, and if you do not have one, you might hold a letter the person wrote (in their handwriting, not typed) or a piece of jewellery or something similar that they possessed. Picking up vibrations in this way is usually described as psychometry, but in this connection I regard the object simply as a link to help your thoughts and feelings on their way. If you have no object to connect you with the person, concentrate on their name.

Communication Spell
Contacting the Dead

Do not attempt this spell out of idle curiosity, maliciousness or because you think it will give you power. If your motive for any spell is selfish or negative, I cannot emphasize strongly enough that it will rebound upon you and in ways which you will find very unpleasant.

Remember also that you cannot harm the dead, they are beyond your reach.

Before commencing this spell, actively indicate the motives and the faith within which you are undertaking it.

If your motive is love (which might also include loss, loneliness, desire to express your feelings or pass on information etc) make sure you have an item as indicated above
which represents the loved one you want to contact.

Do not attempt to contact just anyone, or 'whoever
comes' unless you are trained as a medium, or you will
probably get nothing coherent or useful – in fact, the opposite. It is in cases of this sort where the ouija board or something similar is put to use that the kind of frightening activities involving strange or even malicious energies can make
themselves manifest.

Many people, particularly those who have a strong religious faith, feel that there is something wrong with contacting the spirits of the dead, and the stories which circulate
around the ouija board and the types of energy it appears to
let loose, seem to back up this conviction. But contacting
dead souls is not in itself a wicked or irreligious thing – in
the Bible, for instance, King Saul secretly visited the famed
Witch of Endor to try and get advice from the spirit of the
prophet Samuel. It is only if the attempt is made from the
wrong motives that the results can be frightening or
distressing.

The ouija board – or indeed any other type of open channel which allows inexperienced, often frivolous enquirers
to invite 'anyone there' to come through – can result in
energies which are mischievous, or even harmful, making
their presence felt. Such negative entities are often restless
and have no peaceful place where they belong because of
their selfish and destructive nature. They may be only too
pleased to find themselves invited to make their home
within the unsuspecting personalities at the ouija board,
and once they have a hold, it is very difficult to get rid of
them.

The way that such possession, haunting or overshadowing actually works is not as is popularly believed. Such entities that arrive if summoned in whatever way from beyond
the grave can, if contacted by a medium of integrity or if

summoned in love and trust and in the protection of faith – for whatever positive reason – do no harm and can be instructed when the communication is over to return safely to their own realm and their place in the spirit world. But the kind of entities which crash through an open channel like a ouija board are not necessarily personalities, people who once lived. They are more usually intensifications of energy (generally negative, as I have said) which clamp themselves on to a host personality and refuse to be dislodged. In such a case, the weak and negative aspects of that personality will become intensified – and often the negative force which is strongest within a personality is *fear*. This is why enquirers often become afraid when the affair seems to get out of control. There is in fact nothing to fear – *except the fear itself*.

In my work I have come across many cases where people have had a frightening experience with a ouija board or some other attempt to contact the dead. Generally, they keep the details to themselves, and are reluctant to talk about what happened, unless they turn it into a spooky tale to thrill friends. But it is not the spirits of the dead which cause the trouble, rather the arrogance of the unskilled in the arts of crossing into other worlds which makes them frighten themselves and then blame the souls who are perfectly peaceably minding their own business in their own realms. It is often not appreciated that, while everyone would expect that a climber of high mountains, for example, or a deep sea diver, will need training, skills and equipment before tackling such specialized places, anyone who, like the Wise Woman, habitually journeys into the various hells and heavens of the spirit, including the realms of the dead, has spent years, knowingly or unknowingly, developing the strength and power – and ability – which enables her to do it. Just as no tourist in swimming-trunks would take a deep breath and then make a dive of 20,000 feet without expecting to run into serious trouble, so no one lacking experience or knowledge of the realms of the dead and what might be encountered there can seriously imagine they can spend a spare evening twiddling departed spirits round their fingers and then casually putting them away with the board. The tourist in his swimming-trunks would be dead. The deep-breathers hovering over the board could be – out of the same sort of ignorance – inflicting serious damage upon themselves, perhaps their physical beings, perhaps their souls.

There are, alternatively, some people who are natural, if untrained mediums, and these too can find the situation frightening. So to anyone who is keeping an unnerving experience to himself, thus hanging on to the negativity; or if you find you are receiving information without trying; or do not know how to cope with what is happening, the best place to go for advice, help and healing is, in the first instance, your nearest Spiritualist Church.

Communication Spell (*continued*)

Returning to our Communication Spell: Regarding the protective faith in which you are making your attempt to communicate, have near you or hold in your hand a symbol of that faith – whether a cross, a pentacle or Star of David, the name of Allah or the image of the Buddha, or even an object like a stone or flower which to you is in some way sanctified and makes you feel safe and protected, in touch with a greater power.

Sit somewhere quiet, where you will not be disturbed.

Have near you the personal and sacred objects mentioned above, and a blue or green candle, lighting it before you begin. Green is the colour associated with the heart chakra, the seat of all love, physical and spiritual. If you feel you are prompted by your love, choose this colour candle. Blue is the colour of healing, of mental and physical wholeness. If the person you wish to contact suffered a lot of pain or seemed to endure a difficult life, and you feel you are prompted by a wish to assist in their healing and free them from 'dis-ease' as they progress in the spirit; also to heal yourself of distressing and painful memories, choose a blue candle.

When you are ready, sit with your candle burning and mentally picture the person you wish to contact. Imagine that they have quietly entered the room (leave the door slightly open if possible) and are sitting with you. If you do not know what they looked like, concentrate on their 'essence', the self which is summed up in their name.

When you feel you are ready, speak to them aloud or silently. Thank them for coming, and give them your message, the sentences you have prepared to say – or if you cannot frame them, your emotions and feelings. If you have nothing particular to say at any given time, then do not try to summon the dead. Even in physical existence, people are rightly irritated if called on what seems urgent business, only to find the matter trivial or non-existent. The dead are not harmed if contacted, but they may have to make a great effort to respond, and no medium with a sense of responsibility will undertake to call spirits unnecessarily or have them popping in and out like characters in a French farce, for no good reason.

Neither is it a good idea to call the spirit of a relative, say, just to complain how unhappy you are and moan about your lot. I have known cases where the spirits reacted to this sort of thing very much in the way they would have done if still alive, exasperatedly administering the equivalent of a few well-chosen words before expressing a wish to return to their own realms and remove themselves from the self-pitying caller.

Genuine deep feeling, bereavement, grief, distress, and the fears and angers that are associated with loss and death, may also prevent the person who wishes to make contact from being able to formulate an actual message. This does not matter so long as the unloading of the burden of emotion is felt to be productive rather than negative. Grief and its related problems need to be acknowledged and to be worked through, but the process can sometimes take years. So long as progress of a sort is being made, however, and the mourner is not clinging blindly to the past or wallowing in misery, guilt or similar states of mind, a sorting out of the emotional threads may be painful but can, in the end, only help to develop strength and courage to face the future.

Many people have told me they feel frightened at the thought of speaking to the dead. They anticipate something 'black magicky' or 'witchy' (their words whatever they may mean) which will upset them. But if there is any fear, any distress, any sensation of being threatened or subjected to terror or evil, the whole project is being tackled in the wrong way or for the wrong reasons.

If the contact is attempted in love, trust and faith, in the protection in which you believe and with a sense of full responsibility, the experience may be strange or unexpected, but it will not be frightening. I have known aborted, difficult or awkward connections with dead spirits, tempers and sulks, refusals from the dead to cooperate, but never, without exception, any evil terrors. I have, however, seen sitters leave the session transfigured, shining-eyed, with a radiance and peace about them that comes from the experience they have undergone which has provided certain knowledge that love is stronger than death, and that there are greater and more infinite glories than we can glimpse in our day to day living.

There are two basic emotions which exist in the human mind – love and fear. They cannot exist together, and each will cancel out the other. So if we are fearful we cannot know the full wonder of love and live entirely by it; but if we are filled with love, there is no room left for fear.

When you have finished your session, whatever form it takes, it is necessary to make sure the spirit returns to its own realms. It is impossible to predict exactly what you will experience. Your session may give you the feeling that the person you wished to contact is nearby, no more than that. Or you may deliver your message in trust and love, seemingly into thin air, with little or no reply. Sometimes there is a strong sense of an unspoken message returning to you; loved ones occasionally leave tokens of their presence, moving an object somewhere or managing a gentle, unseen touch. Unless you are a natural medium, it is unlikely, especially at the beginning, that you will 'hear' sentences or be able to speak directly in conversation, but it is amazing how people who have lived with and loved each other can provide their own very individual messages. Do not treat such occurrences as coincidence – if you have longed for a communication from someone close to you, and such a thing appears to come, accept it for what it is. The spirits are restricted in the ways in which they can communicate, and they often make use of private, significant words, names, songs and other such things which will mean a great deal to you, and nothing much to anyone else.

At the end of the session, say goodbye to whichever spirits might be present, and once again thank them for coming. Tell them that it is time for them to return to the place from which they have come to you, and (if you wish to do so) promise to speak to them again. Then sit quietly for a few moments until you feel you are alone once more. Blow out your candle as a sign that the communication is at an end.

Meditation from Ancient Wisdom
Beyond the Grave

Though the seas overflow and the rivers burst their banks, yet many waters cannot quench us, for we are indestructible and in our weakness is our strength. Upon our brows we carry the stars and the moons are beneath our feet. As the eternal seams of rock are a part of each other, so our handclasp will wear away only in aeons of winter rain and the droughts of summer. We are indivisible for there is no seam and the fabric was woven by one loom.

We are a garden of flowers of which there are many blooms yet all enclosed within the same high wall. We are the colours in a prism of light that are all different and dart their separate ways

64

and can never meet or be the same and yet are part of the whole. We have died, separately so that we may know what it is to live, together.

We shall go forward together and still the waters to make a path. We shall read the stones and place the patterns of the clouds and the rippling of the rivers together so that all will be clear. We shall open the gates.

Do not fear. Fear is the crying of children in the dark. The dark is but empty space. There is nothing to fear. You yourselves are the light and carry within you suns and moons. I am the torchbearer to touch your lights into flame. This is only the beginning. There will be no end.

4

The Wild Path

When we think of early civilizations – Ancient Egyptians, for instance, or the Incas – the temptation is to dwell on their picturesque, romantic qualities, the robes and feathers and gold enamelled masks and jewels, the excitingly barbaric thrill of the fact that they were so different from nineties man and woman. This temptation also applies to the Celts. We recognize that they were pagan but we gloss over what that really meant and turn them into a sort of cloak-swirling culture of silver-tongued hippies, into nature and making rather bold jewellery out of pebbles and having a natural gift for musical instruments like the harp.

'We even demand that the ancient Celts think like modern Westerners,' as R.J. Stewart points out in *Celtic Gods, Celtic Goddesses.*

Stop to consider that for a moment. The ancient Celts were not modern, or even westerners, they had come from the barbaric East originally, and they had no framework of Sunday being a 'day of rest', or even regular attendance at the synagogue or the mosque. Their thought processes (as R.J. Stewart is quick to point out) were not even similar to those of the Romans, with whom we can at least identify logically.

In the same manner, the spiritual power of Native

American Indian cultures is often incomprehensible to us once we have passed beyond the novelty of the pipe of peace, the totem pole, the wampum beads and the tepee. It can, in realistic fact, be very frightening, scalping and torture seeming to be far more typical of the culture than joy or reassurance in the shamanistic mysteries.

The Celts were just as barbaric, just as seemingly incomprehensible to modern eyes. Seemingly just as frightening. In this chapter we will examine some of their wilder aspects and see what we can learn from them in this age when the world seems to have gone mad, and far more subtle and sophisticated cruelties, barbarities and indifference to the beautiful and the good – the truth itself – can be found on every page of a modern newspaper.

The Headhunters

It is noticeable that Celtic tales and legends are filled with magical signs, symbols and such items as the head of the hero Bendigeid Vran (Bran the Blessed), which might well be described by the irreverent as 'all-singing, all-dancing'. The head was, at Bran's own instruction, ritually cut off by his followers after he had been wounded by a poisoned spear while struggling with the enemy Irish. Again at his instruction, it was carried on a long drawn out journey around Britain for eighty years, to be buried finally at the White Hill (probably Tower Hill) in London with the face turned towards France. During this time it prophesied, gave advice to his old friends, and sang most sweetly.

This seems a very odd story, not to say gruesome, but the preoccupation with the magical head springs from the fact that the Celts laid great store by heads. They were literally headhunters, and there are shelves of rock still in existence with niches where the severed heads could be stored.

Not a great deal is known about this aspect of their lives, though there is plenty of archaeological evidence that stone heads, as well as the real thing, held great significance for them and were used widely as decoration and also symbolically. The decapitated heads of enemies were fixed to the bridles of Celtic warriors, and preserved in cedar oil. They served in many mysterious and sacred ways – as tokens of prowess, as trophies and power sources, or totems. The Celts believed that the energy of the slain warrior would magically be absorbed by the victor, and also that the ghost of the dead man, once his head was cut off, would be rendered harmless, unable to return again either in a physical body or a spiritual one.

Apart from the significance of the severed head as a war trophy, however, there was a much deeper meaning to it, and skulls were used for sacred purposes. This emphasis on the sanctity of the head came largely from two sources, both of which can, in a less dramatic manner, hold relevance today. One was shamanistic, the other concerned the cult of the dead and the worship of ancestors.

Message of the Heroes

The Celtic traditions lay great stress on what can be described as ancestor worship, but it was not so much for the individual, but rather for the gods or the heroes of race myth and legend, who weaved a magical pattern in and out of both the physical and the spiritual worlds, inspiring and encouraging the ordinary mortal. Most religions acknowledge, even if they do not accentuate, that the dead can be contacted in some way, and will generally respond if the need is great enough. But the immense chasm between the living world and the world of the dead must, of its own nature, be mysterious, difficult to bridge and filled with dangers for those who are not empowered to cross it.

To the Celts – and to many other believers in other places and other cultures – the spirits of dead ancestors and the spirits of the deities they worshipped were mystically linked, so much so that the myths and traditions featured great father and mother god and goddess figures who were supposedly common ancestors of all. There is no absolute divinity in Celtic belief, and therefore no creed of sin and punishment, based on an attempt to achieve perfection. The Celts were not religious in that way. The magical entities they acknowledged were perceived in everything around them, particularly in natural phenomena, and they were highly superstitious, attempting through their rituals to propitiate these fearsome and powerful beings.

The ancestor/heroes of Celtic myth were not gods, but they somehow managed to reach an almost divine status. Take the characters of the great Irish folk legends, and the Welsh tales in the *Mabinogion* – the name of which is taken from Mabon, the mysterious, half-divine Son in Celtic belief, who, imprisoned in the dark of an underground tomb, overcomes the dark through sacrifice and with his own shining light; these characters probably never actually lived at all in the ways in which they are presented, far less performed the feats which are chronicled in the stories. Yet in Celtic lore, the heroes are real, their tragedies and victories and struggles endear them to us because of their very human weaknesses and frailty. Finn and Olwen, Arthur and Branwen, Lancelot and Deirdre, are a part of those who are spiritually Celtic, as much an inspiration as our own actual dead, and as loved.

This sense of belonging, of feeling one's roots reach back even into the dimmest past, can have a very positive effect, one which is particularly needed at a time when the traditional social values, the unity of the family itself, the sense of participating in an eternal grand chain of life, handing what has been passed down to us on to others, appears to be becoming broken and fragmented. A consciousness only of self, of callous greed and disregard, of a jungle mentality that, far from wanting to protect the weak, regards them as prey, seems to be the unhappy philosophy which is, however unwantedly, flourishing like bindweed within western society as the end of the millennium approaches.

What the Celts allegedly lived by in this respect, based on the inspiration and example of their ancestors, can say a lot to us today. How is anyone to be fully aware of who they are, where they have come from and where they are going, if they are emotionally adrift and do not feel any sense of belonging through family or tribal roots?

There is further evidence of the value of this way of thinking. Celtic belief was singularly free of a religious sense of duty and service, and consequently of social rebellion and guilt, but the culture is generally recognized to have been spontaneously caring. Though there were classes within the tribal system, the Celts were apparently unusually enlightened towards those among them who could not help themselves – the old, the weak and particularly (most unusually in ancient and pagan cultures) the mentally ill as well as the physically sick. It is said that they cared for their sick and weak in special 'hospices', and placed such importance on this service that they regularly ran tests to weed out quack doctors and healers. Any healers who did not meet the prescribed standards were severely dealt with. A gentle hint for the health authorities of today, perhaps?

A Building, not a Breaking

In the pre-Christian days, the Celts used skulls as sacred drinking vessels at shrines, and the severed trophy heads were hung over doorways for protection. But we can use the awareness of the power, inspiration and comfort of all who have gone before us, without chopping off heads. There is a time for everything, and just as there was a time for a 'breaking up' – indeed, seemingly there has always been a time for breaking things up – so there is a time for building. Looking at the world around us, it seems that if that time has not actually arrived, it is only just around the corner.

71

But we cannot turn ourselves, just like that, into great heroic figures, take sword in hand and go out on the 8.40 to slay a few dragons. People often feel helpless, believing that it will make little difference if one person tries to make a stand. But think of the way the Celts worked their spells in this respect; they took on the responsibility for the weak, the sick, the old. They worked out a system; they cared. If just one person takes on that sort of responsibility willingly, within his own personal world, however limited, and makes it work cheerfully and without carping all the time about 'compensation' and 'rights', something positive has been achieved. And positivity is never lost. Amazingly enough, the person who makes the effort will also find his own life transformed. Remember what we said earlier, that you will get back only what you give? This works positively as well as negatively.

Meditation from the Bible
(Ecclesiastes 3:1-8)

To every thing there is a season, and a time to every purpose under the heaven:

A time to be born, and a time to die; a time to plant, and a time to pluck up that which is planted;

A time to kill, and a time to heal; a time to break down, and a time to build up;

A time to weep, and a time to laugh; a time to mourn, and a time to dance;

A time to cast away stones, and a time to gather stones together; a time to embrace, and a time to refrain from embracing;

A time to get, and a time to lose; a time to keep, and a time to cast away;

A time to rend, and a time to sew; a time to keep silence, and a time to speak;

A time to love, and a time to hate; a time of war, and a time of peace.

Totem Animals – Their Secret Power

It was a part of the Celtic belief that the natural world reflected the magic and power of Celtic deities, animals often belonging to certain gods or goddesses. This is sometimes represented as a rather naïve anthropomorphic idea, or a cosy generality, suggesting that we (including animals) are all part of one big happy pagan family. In fact, the complexity of Celtic belief cannot be explained as simply as that, though animals were important to them. But the ways in which they let animal forms link them with their gods, or reveal secrets of spiritual truth through the shamanistic rituals performed by the Druids, can open up new vision and strength to us now.

Letting animals play a part in your living, not just as pampered pets, but as a personal source of strength and inspiration, is very Celtic. The Celts not only linked animals to their gods, but regarded them symbolically as representatives of different aspects of nature and the land, the kingdom – even of different qualities of character, nobility and heroism. It is enough just to know that, by identifying with your own totem animal or bird (at this stage, in however superficial a way) you can open up your daily life, your dreams and your awareness and feel that the world of nature is with you and you are a part of it.

Finding your Totem Animal

1. You will need to sit quietly, where you know you will not be disturbed for at least half an hour.

2. Relax, concentrate on your breathing, listen to your breath passing in and out gently and evenly through the nose for several minutes.

3. Continuing to concentrate on your breathing, allow your eyes to shut and imagine yourself sitting in the warm dark of a cave in winter-time. It is peaceful and safe, you are

comfortable and well fed.

4. Be aware that outside the cave is the wild Celtic world, deep forests, unscaleable mountain peaks, the silence of the depths of winter under snow. Your totem animal or bird or creature – whatever it is – has guided you here to rest safely, and awaits you outside the cave. It belongs in this world of nature, it understands it and is a part of it. You have been unaware in your present life, but your animal guide has been beside you always, an unseen companion.

5. When you feel ready, visualize yourself pulling your furs round you and moving mentally to the mouth of the cave. There is light outside. Is it daylight? Sunlight? Moonlight? Firelight? Identify what you see.

6. Do not hurry nor be surprised at what you find. When you can see the light, visualize yourself looking round for the companion which has been awaiting you. It may be large – a horse, a bull, or an animal you would not have expected like a tiger or a buffalo or ancient mastodon, perhaps a large animal you do not recognize. Do not attempt to change what you see to suit the idea of what you expected or wanted to see.

7. The animal may be small, and out of its rightful element. A snake, a squirrel, a mouse. It will, in true animal fashion, keep its distance, even though it is aware of you and is waiting for you.

8. If you do not see anything, be patient and look closer. There may be a bird on a nearby tree branch, waiting quietly. There may be a spider's web, dripping with jewelled light, spun between two branches.

9. Mentally ask your guide and companion to identify itself in some way. When you think you have been given a sign, speak to your totem animal. Thank it for being there and tell it you accept it and will welcome its guidance and strength in your life.

10. If you cannot see anything, keep trying through successive sessions of visualization, without feeling any pressure. Some people need to practise their visualization,

or the spirits may be testing you in some way. Even if nothing seems to happen, you will benefit from the meditation and relaxation.

11. When your visualization is complete, tell your totem animal you wish to leave it and return to the world in which you are sitting, but that you will come back and speak to it further. Then visualize yourself going back into the cave, sitting peacefully and safely, and letting the cave drift away so that you are able to open your eyes once more relaxed in your chair.

Being aware of your totem animal opens up previously closed areas in your mind. You will sense its reassuring presence around you, and begin to feel more sure of your own strengths and weaknesses – for instance, size, brawn or physical beauty is not always the best thing to assist in survival in the animal kingdom. Cunning, persistence or an ability to adapt can prove far more useful and effective in the end. So even if your ideal totem is something familiar and traditionally good-looking like a saluki dog or black cat, you may, after your initial dismay, find that the frog or snake which presents itself to you has far more to offer than any doggy or moggy! Totem animals have quite different properties from pets – they are more in the nature of lucky pieces, reminders and guides of ways to go, realistic – though symbolic – reinforcings of your own personal strength and good qualities.

Here are a few brief notes on some possible totem animals:

Horse The horse was the totem animal of the great Earth Goddess herself. Kings of mediaeval Ireland were traditionally ritually 'married to a mare', this noble creature representing the power and fertility of the land. The goddess known as Epona (from which comes our word for 'pony'), the Welsh Rhiannon and the Irish Macha were all horse goddesses.

The horse has always lived and worked closely with man, lending its superior strength in peace and in war, a servant and yet a beloved friend and companion, with the usefulness of a human being and with the difference of its untamed animal heritage. White horses herald the coming of the mysteries, and carry the knight in search of the dragons and the Grail. Mystic animals will emerge from the white horses of the sea which thunder on to the sand.

The 'hobby horse' of old English ritual represents the ancient belief that the goddess was transformed into a mare at certain times, and throughout history horses have been among man's most valued possessions, prized beyond price.

The horse will bring you: companionship, magic, the ability to travel into other realms, loyalty and faithfulness.

Spider Do not fear the image of the long-legged spider, for this is one of the most magical of creatures. The Welsh goddess Arianrhod carries her starry weaver's shuttle along with other spidery women of myth. In Greek legend, Arachne challenged the goddess Athena to a contest of spinning – and won. In fury, Athena transformed the girl into a spider, condemned to spin for ever – with the name 'arachnid'! Ariadne saved the hero Theseus from the labyrinth after he killed the Minotaur (the foundations of the very same labyrinth are in Crete) by guiding him safely through with her spidery thread; while Penelope unpicked the tapestry she had woven each night in order to halt the passing of time until her husband Ulysses returned to her from Troy. (He did not come back for another ten years.)

It is the task of the Fates – usually a group of three old crones or magical weird sisters to spin the symbolic thread that makes up the fabric of each individual's life, from birth to death. The grimmest of the sisters holds a pair of shears and has the power to cut the thread when life is to end.

There is a lovely tale that when Mary and Joseph were fleeing into Egypt they were forced to hide from the soldiers who were seeking the baby Jesus. A small spider, industriously spinning a web across the corner where they cowered, hid them and so saved the child. Even now, the ordinary garden spider still carries a cross on its back in recognition of this service.

There are many in the animal kingdom who are marked because of their sacrifice, often traditionally to Christ. One of the explanations for the robin's red breast, for instance, is that the bird was helping to carry the gift of fire to humanity from the sun, and held on to the burning brand too long; but another story attributes the red colour to blood, rather than fire. The robin was marked, it is said, while trying to pluck the thorns from the head of the dying Christ. As a totem animal, the robin brings nothing but good, the ability to survive hardship, compassion and courage, the ability to make sacrifices in the face of general need, a small steady light that flickers on even if all the other lights of the world seem to be fading.

Returning to the spider, she will bring you: cosmic awareness of the patterns of life and death; industry and persistence; a sense of fate and destiny; creativity and skilled craftsmanship; good luck. Here are some words from the Goddess: *Without love there would be a dark void where the hounds of Chaos roam in their packs, baying to the light of a black moon. The strands of love are like the strands of the web spun by the celestial spider that reach out across the galaxies, linking planet to planet and the souls of the tiny insects to their counterparts. Love touches like the flake of snow, in its crystalline beauty, which brings stars to rest upon the foreheads of mortal men.*

Owl The owl's two chief attributes are as a possessor of ancient wisdom, and as a portent of doom. Both of these are probably erroneous. As the owner and handler of a white owl once remarked to me: 'The owl's reputation for wisdom comes from its stillness and wide stare. In fact, all it is doing is listening so hard that it can pinpoint exactly where its prey is moving. Then, in one swoop, it gets dinner over with and can relax until the next day. No special skills at hunting, no clever thinking at all – unless the way it concentrates on pinpointing its dinner and dealing with it shows sense.'

Just as erratic is the owl's reputation as a bad luck bringer. If you see an owl at practically any time, or hear it in the morning, noon or night, indoors or out, all of these will, according to tradition, signify doom in various ways. And yet, anyone who has had the privilege of being close to one of these creatures, and looked deep into the wide, wild eyes, will not doubt for a moment that they have been in the presence of something ancient and wonderful.

The Celtic heritage of the owl is filled with glorious magic that can transform this bird – one of the oldest creatures living on the earth, traditionally – as it was itself transformed. In the *Mabinogion*, the hero Llew, cursed never to marry a mortal, was presented by his magician uncles with a bride who had been created from 'flowers of oak, meadowsweet and broom'. She was called Blodeuwedd, 'the flower-faced one' and was utterly enchanting. However, in the way of magical beings she was unable to remain faithful to her husband, and took a lover, with whom she plotted to kill the infatuated Llew.

As a punishment, one of her creators turned her into an owl – and her name is the Welsh word for that bird.

The owl will bring you: the ability to see opportunities and to take them; ruthless self analysis; detachment; calamitous beauty; simplicity; presence and purpose to move forward.

Snake From legends of fearful dragons and sea-serpents to the poisonous adders of Albion (Ancient Britain), the snake has made, perhaps, the greatest impact ever on man from the point of view of reputation and image. It has had both a good and a bad reputation, has always been considered magical and because it is so different from a human being it has always been viewed with awe.

In ancient Rome, snakes were kept as pets – 'house snakes' – to guard the home, and the snake's beneficial influence is illustrated in its appearance on the caduceus, the symbol generally recognized as that of medicine and healing. There is a whole tradition of snake-lore, from 'adder stones' used to heal cataracts, to 'snake-stones' which the Druids used in their rites.

Generally though, the snake has had a very bad press and has never quite managed to live down its activities in the Garden of Eden – it has since been regarded as a schemer, troublemaker and all-round undesirable, not to be trusted. But the Celts recognized the snake for its power, and immortalized it in jewellery that clasped the neck or breast in the form of a snake with ram's, or horned heads. These heavy bracelets and torques are of typically Celtic design, though similar snake jewellery, usually signifying protective power, can be found in other cultures. The snake has always been one of the most powerful symbols of the natural world.

The healing properties of the snake are endless, though the ingredients might be difficult to obtain today. Snakeskin and associated items such as adder's venom reputedly cure anything from eye problems, headaches and rheumatism to unwanted pregnancies. Snakes also preside over the mysteries of the childbed as creatures of the Celtic goddess Brigid.

The snake will bring you: secrecy and sensuality, sexual control and power, renewal and long-term survival, an ability to accept and transform the pains of growth and progression.

Cat Cats were in the past considered threatening, sinister and disturbing, but largely because they possessed supernatural properties of prophecy and divination, and could work all manner of magic. They were worshipped in ancient Egypt as the cat goddess Bast, and cats were considered to play a more important part in ancient Egyptian households than the human members of the family. They wielded immense power, and the part they played in the Celtic world is not at all that of the domestic feline purring by the fire. Cat flesh (along with the flesh of a 'red pig' or a dog) was stipulated for magical or prophetic Otherworld banquets, and Celtic myth contains tales of cat monsters, cat giants and other cat nuisances who had to be hunted out and destroyed by King Arthur and his knights.

The cat has always been magical, and this probably explains why the ordinary person can become rather nervous in its presence. The cat walks alone, its power is not shared with others, and it commands obedience while giving nothing in return. This secrecy reflects in its connection with Frejya, the Scandinavian goddess of the moon, who rode in a chariot that was pulled by gigantic cats.

Often in the past, cats have been considered to bring bad luck because of their ability to sense and give forewarning of floods, storms, underground dangers and general disaster.

The cat will bring you: pride in independence, secret knowledge, psychic ability; grace and flexibility; good luck; individuality, flair and self-containment.

The Shamanistic Experience

To some extent, the Celts followed shamanistic practices – the wise man was wrapped within the freshly flayed hide of a bull, for instance, so that he might, in his trance and prophetic utterances, take on the qualities of the bull in natural magic to assist him on his journeyings into and out of the Otherworld.

Initiation as a shaman involves overcoming death, so that the spirit of the shaman can walk in all realms of life and death and return safely to the body to use his or her experiences and power wisely. There are ceremonies of initiation, but it can occur spontaneously as it did with

Yvaine Huath, another wise and very experienced Celtic psychic and mystic.

'It was at one very low point in my life,' she told me. 'I knew I had, or was something, but it was in a very painful way. I had tried suicide before, since I found living very difficult, as though I did not belong in the world. I did not really want to die, but I felt I could not live, I felt alienated, I was very depressed and desperately afraid I was becoming insane. I shut myself up for "as long as it took", whatever would happen, and spent the days trying to find my realities and journey deep into myself to reach my soul. I did not then realize I was clairvoyant, that I had the psychic powers and so on. I was very tired, very afraid.'

'It seems like a great step in the dark,' I prompted, and she nodded.

'Oh, yes. But there was no other way, you see. And I think the shamanic initiation has to come in some way from the negative feelings of disgust and fear, complete loneliness, an awareness that it might be death which happens and a giving up of the ego to the great power, even when you are not aware of the nature of that power.'

'What happened?'

'I came through it. I had visions of the ultimate bliss, union with the Absolute, which is utterly incredible and changes your whole perception of life and death; I crossed the barriers between life and death, spent some time suspended between them. This does not involve "nearly dying" or suffering a "near-death experience" but more a shift of attitude. It was painful – I was physically ill and exhausted and it was far more frightening than anything I had ever imagined, though, in a strange sort of way, the whole process is like a recognition. As though, I suppose, the channels within, and between me and the other worlds, the other planes, the awareness, came into focus and I knew that was how I was, and how it had to be.'

'It must have been frightening for your partner, Noel. What did he feel about it?'

Yvaine half-smiled.

'Well, he had already accepted, as everyone else in my life had, that I was "different" in some way. And I think he understood that there was no other way – I mean, I literally had no choice, I was driven, though without knowing where or what for, to that period apart and alone, and it was something that had been building up all the years I was alive, though I was not aware of it. He was worried, I think, but he was very supportive, and let me do it my way. In many ways, we shared the journey, and it affected him a great deal as well. We talked things over, and I told him what I had experienced – he became closer to me, stronger in himself, more able to communicate, though he is not psychic himself, or very spiritual.'

A Shape-shifting Spell

'Shape-shifting', the ability to change shape, to deceive the eye, to look different, is present often not only in the rituals of Celtic shamanism, but in the myths, closely linked with rich and symbolic stories of the Otherworld.

And today, we can 'shape-shift' too. The desire to get a make-over in some shape or form, whether to invest in a different hairstyle, new clothes or a whole fresh and unexpected personal image can be reasonably painlessly achieved. This desire is not, as nonconformist tradition would have us believe, an expression of sinful vanity, but a form of recharging the magical energies that drive us through this life. The confidence of an attractive new hairstyle can enable the shy and the timid to astound others by speaking out, making their presence felt, attaining new poise and dignity. Such 'shapeshifting' carries its own particular brand of magic, and is one of the simplest spells you can cast to improve all the areas of your life.

Having your body – or nose, even – recreated by plastic surgeons can help in extreme cases, but it is better to just make the most of what you were born with. After all, even Cleopatra had a too-long nose, but she was far too busy coping with her hectic love-life to spare the time for a beautifying 'nose job'. But if you do not feel comfortable within your skin because you perceive yourself as a bedraggled, frowsty hen, your choice for improvement is literally limitless. It involves only a shift in attitude, an imaginative approach and – most important of all – a belief in the magic.

Who could possibly want to carry on clucking round the farmyard when they might be tantalizing their family and associates as an enigmatic, sapphire-eyed Siamese cat? Or gliding through their days with the rainbow-tinted grace of a dragonfly?

All is possible in the Celtic world.

The Language of Magic

ii

Chakras The chakras are the energy points of the body, according to many systems of healing including Japanese Reiki. In actual fact, the body is covered with energy points, but when referring to 'the chakras', it is usually understood that seven particular ones are meant. These form a rough line down the spine, the length of the body. They cannot be seen with the eye, but psychics or experienced practitioners can sense, feel and work on them to balance them and unblock knotted energy within the body so that it flows freely. They are referred to as follows: The **crown chakra** – at the top of the head, through which energy enters the body and through which the spirit leaves and returns, connected by a silver cord if the body still lives – as in dreams, out of body or near death experiences. When the body dies, the spirit leaves and the cord is severed. The **third eye** – this is between the brows. It is the seat of meditative and spiritual awareness. To develop it, wear a lapis lazuli. The deep blue colour is the colour of this chakra. The **throat chakra** – at the base of the throat. Problems of expressing the truth, of putting true feelings into words, are typical of the difficulties that can be encountered here. The **heart chakra** – at heart level in the mid-chest. The green colour signifies love both spiritual and physical, for the heart is where the spirit meets the physical. To encourage the heart chakra to open, wear the crystals of rose quartz or kunzite. To stabilize emotional balance use emerald or malachite. The **solar plexus chakra** – just above the navel. This is concerned with feelings and emotions – the so-called 'gut reaction' and 'gut instinct'. To encourage the body to replenish energy and keep the 'gut reaction' healthy, wear the brilliant yellow of the citrine or topaz. The **sacral chakra** – situated on the spine at the level of the sacrum. The element present in this chakra is water. The fluidity, the plumpening, the ripening necessary for physical and bodily life is present here, also the fluid essence that allows a healthy sexual existence. Keep this chakra protected by the carnelian, the stone that represents the life force – this is also the place to protect yourself against colds and allergies. The carnelian or ruby lends the fire of life. The **root chakra** – at the base of the spine. This roots us to the earth and to the reality of physical existence. Without a good base we are not properly grounded. Anxiety can spring from feeling unsafe with regard to our position in the physical world. Use bloodstone or garnet to assist, and black tourmaline or haematite to help you feel you are firmly 'touching base'.

Otherworld There are three worlds in the Celtic picture of the cosmos, which, along with other similar belief systems, follow what is called the 'chthonic pattern', and can be visualized as three circles, one above the other, intertwining.

The upper world, 'sky world', is the realm of higher forms such as gods and goddesses, reflected in the patterns and movements of the Sun, Moon and Stars. These

Otherworlds are known as Gwynwyd, the white land, with above it, Ceugant, the heaven or Nirvana.

The middle world 'Earth World' (called Abred) is complicated by the overlapping zones of the circles, but is largely much as we would imagine our Earth to be, with mysterious areas of spirit presences and primal fears that reflect the three levels of psychological awareness.

The lower Underworld (Annwyn) is the dark world of death and rebirth, ruled by its own shadowy gods. Here also dwell the spirits of ancestors, and there are links with the stars.

Ouija board A method particularly popular during the twenties and thirties of making contact with dead spirits. It consists of a board with the letters of the alphabet surrounding the edge and, at opposite sides, the words 'yes' and 'no'. A pointer called a planchette rests in the centre – sometimes an upturned tumbler is used instead. Enquirers sit round the board, a fingertip of each resting on the planchette very lightly. The board is asked specific questions, and the planchette or tumbler moves (supposedly without being pushed) round the circle of letters to spell out its message.

This is advertised as a spooky parlour game rather than a serious psychic or mediumistic aid (but see my comments earlier.)

5

How to Get What You Want

Take what you want and pay for it, says God.
                                    Spanish proverb.

Then since her love for the Prince was so great, she braved
the lonely, dark path to where the wise woman lived, and
knocked with trembling hands.
    'Who is there, and what do you want from me?' the wise
woman asked from the shadows.
    'I want to be mortal,' whispered the possessor of eternal
life, in all her youth and fairy beauty. 'I want to live and die
with my Prince and be buried in the same grave with him.'
    The wise woman's unfaltering eyes regarded her with
understanding and pity.
    'I will give you the philtre. But the price you must pay is
high.'
    'What is the price?' the immortal breathed.
    'You will become the possessor of a human soul,' said
the wise woman.
                                    Yvaine Huath

Do not wish too hard for what you want – you might get it.
                                    Old proverb.

People who consult a Wise Woman – as opposed to those
who have their fortune told in a spirit of fun – almost
always want something. Souls at peace with themselves
and others, content with their circumstances and prospects,
have neither the time nor the inclination to make a point of
approaching someone else with their desires and asking
whether they will achieve them. But such well-balanced
people are rare, and following on love and death, the next

preoccupation is desire, and the means by which desires can be attained.

Hardly anyone is happy, satisfied with his lot, without a vague sensation that something is missing. Most people suggest rather cynically that 'money helps you to be miserable in comfort', and in the same way as a previous generation hoped for their lives to be transformed by the treble chance in the football pools, thousands of people are now, quite literally staking their hopes of a future on the national lottery.

It is all very well to point out that the odds are millions to one. If people feel their lives are empty or lacking, it is their need and sense of lack that matters most, and practically everyone who consults a wise woman – or equally, consults a psychiatrist or a priest of any religion – wants something. Often they do not know what it is.

On the Side of the Big Battalions

The Celts, as we have heard, were dedicated warriors, renowned for their skill in battle. It was reported that as a race, they were 'war-mad', brimming over with energy, vitality, readiness to get to grips with situations they did not find agreeable. They did not sit about bewailing the invasion of their territory, but engaged in guerilla warfare and spectacularly drove out all comers, even the highly sophisticated might of the Roman armies. And what they wanted, they took. If they had to pay the price for divine intervention on their behalf – as Boudicca paid the human sacrifices demanded by the fierce and bloody Andrasta – they settled. Their men were heroes all, not a balding, overweight wimp among them; their women were anything from wonderfully beautiful to the most ferocious of hags, but each one vibrant with life, sure of herself and making her wants and her opinions known in no uncertain terms.

It was Voltaire who commented that God is on the side of

the big battalions. Napoleon, an arch go-getter, pointed out that an army marches on its stomach. Both of these remarks make sense, and underline the fact that wispy ideals, vague resolves and uncertain spirituality have to give way to practical realism if we are to live in a physical world. In Celtic terms, think of yourself as a warrior. Do not sit about complaining about what is wrong. Do something to improve matters. Remember that, in one well-known phrase: it is better to light a candle than to curse the dark.

The first and most important way to get what you want is to begin *living in the moment*.

There is a past and a future, but the past has always gone, and the future will always be still to come. Essentially there is only the *now*, the present moment, and even if it seems dreary and empty, squalid, poor, with little to look forward to except even worse problems and trials, you have to realize that the moment is all you have. It is where you must begin.

Most people (hopeful lottery millionaires included) are attempting to start getting what they want at some unspecified point in time which might be three and a half years from now, or even twenty-five years ahead. It is important to appreciate that, though it is better (in the words of R.L. Stevenson) to travel hopefully and have something to look forward to, the point in time that you are looking forward to, when things suddenly start to go right for you, will never actually come. You will always be stuck in an eternal '*now*'.

Therefore it follows that you must start from the here and now, creating your own future prosperity for yourself.

Do not wait for tomorrow, hoping things will get better. Unfortunately, they hardly ever do, but you can change, if not your circumstances, certainly your perceptions of them and reactions to them. Quite often, reality is not what we think it is.

Basically, there are three levels of wanting – the material, the emotional and the spiritual. Though most people do not realize it, their wants may, while seeming to be obvious – a white Rolls Royce, a husband, beauty – actually be for something else. What seems material may be emotional, what seems emotional may be spiritual – and it is more than likely that all three levels are in some way involved.

Think of your material wants. They will be either *what you actually need* or *what those needs represent*. And since no-one on this Earth really needs a wardrobe of 300-plus pairs of shoes or ten cars, most 'needs' are irrelevant. It is only possible to wear one outfit of clothes at a time and eat one plateful of food. You cannot inhabit a country estate, town house, villa and yacht simultaneously. Unless you are literally living in a cardboard box and possess only what you stand up in, chances are that you do not really need anything that is not already available to you or which you cannot reasonably obtain. Not, that is, in order to actually live positively in this moment.

Consider the following 'wants':

   a monetary win/windfall
   jewels
   a new car
   a bigger/better house
   antiques/specialized items/rare books/stamps/etc
   a caravan/boat/second or holiday home
   designer clothes/furs
   exotic holiday/trip to a special place
   new kitchen/dishwasher/fridge/loft extension/
       conservatory/etc/etc

In my experience as a psychic counsellor, I have never known sitters ask 'How can I get a new fitted kitchen?' or even 'How can I get an extra bedroom, the children are growing and we need it, so can you do a spell please?' They actually discuss all 'wants' of the kind listed above realistically, even whether to try to change their house for another, or get a mortgage so that they can in other ways expand. They may ask for advice as to what action to take, but the solid necessities of life are recognized by all sitters as removed from the magic of 'I want', and they are usually ready to try to tackle such needs on a practical basis, taking their responsibilities on board themselves.

The exception is the sitter who wants to opt out, and asks how her husband/the children/the rowdy neighbours/her mother-in-law/the rest of the world can be magically transformed into Disneyland, with herself as the Princess. Since she inhabits a world of her own, we will safely leave her there.

It is notable that sitters rarely request clothes or jewels, holidays, cars or antiques in any serious manner. The only 'want' which does occur with boring and predictable frequency is for 'a win on the lottery' or 'money, money, money . . . !'

Make a Pile?

Money represents the answer to everything. It will bring permanent ease and security, purchase companionship, attention, the illusion of youth, respect, the dispelling of fears and emotional difficulties – or so people think.

For this reason, I intended to include here a spell for making or getting huge amounts of money. There are such spells, and there are other practitioners who will oblige you if you ask for them. But as a Wise Woman, I know that when I petition the powers in any way at all about large amounts of money (especially if achieved overnight), they are silent. Guidance is given on which course to take, whether to consult solicitors or other experts in business dealings, the outcome of court cases or insurance claims – and sometimes, though not very often, I have seen great wealth appearing from nowhere for sitters who are not asking for it – but questions like: 'How can I win the lottery/Who'll win the 4.30/Where shall I put the counters on the roulette table' will not be answered.

The reason why this is so is a personal thing, and I cannot speak for other psychics or consultants. But in the role I have been assigned as a Wise Woman, I am aware that – for me, at any rate – it is necessary to live by the spiritual precepts like those given in the Bible: to have the faith to believe that my needs will be taken care of, that I am in the hands of a higher power, that there are more important things than the desire for 'lots of money quickly' and that I will be granted enough to manage (in some way or another) but no more. Most religions incorporate such a letting-go of material concerns, and anyone trying to follow a spiritual path must genuinely be prepared to renounce the world's wealth even if, paradoxically, they then suddenly begin to experience huge amounts of money coming to them and grow so incredibly wealthy that they cannot cope. (This is another matter altogether.)

As a Wise Woman, I am also aware that if people are so obsessed with money that they manage to divert large amounts of it to themselves by means of spells or magic, they are in fact taking something which, in the natural order of things, was not intended for them. And so, as with all magic, they will have to pay for it – probably in a manner that is more painful than the original situation would have been. The spiritual world in its purest form does not concern itself with money for its own sake.

But *riches*? Now that is another matter. There is no spell in this book for making a fast buck, but the following will, in some way or another, bring great richness to your life.

Spells and Magic to Bring Luck, Health and Prosperity

Everything you ever wanted

1. Use the time of the waxing of the moon for bringing things towards you and creating, the waning of the moon for clearing things out, letting go.

2. Use numbers and the power of numerology to assist you. The Celtic world is based on the magical number 3. *'What I tell you three times is true'* (Lewis Carroll).

Find your own personal number (instructions in **Language of Magic iii**) and use it.

3. What is your special colour? There is one which suits your personality and looks better than any other. Wear it and feel yourself come into focus. (See how in **Language of Magic iii**).

4. Let gem stones enrich you. Each sign of the zodiac has its own special gem, but they can often be very general, so choose your personal particular favourites to wear as well.

Aries (March 21-April 20) Diamond, bloodstone, garnet. Aries is strength and fire, expressed in the colour red (bloodstone and garnet) and the fact that diamond is traditionally the hardest of all gem stones.

Taurus (April 21-May 20) Rose quartz. Taurus is an Earth sign, comfort means a lot and possessions are valued. Taurus lives sensibly in the reality of the present, and the rose quartz (as we have seen) echoes feelings of self-worth and satisfaction, appreciating that life is good.

Gemini (May 21-June 21) Agate. In all its colours and forms, the agate stone balances all levels of existence, physical, mental and spiritual, bringing calmness and peace. The Gemini twins of this sign, the two sides of Gemini's personality and nature, are thus reconciled with each other.

Cancer (June 22-July 23) Moonstone, clear crystal and any white-coloured stones. This Water sign reflects its thoughtful changes of mood in the delicate transparency of crystal, with the moonstone signifying hidden depths, links with past and future.

Leo (July 24-August 23) Catseye and chrysolite. The

warmth of a deep lion-hug surrounds the Leo subject and radiates outwards on to everyone else. Tawny stones that give off sunlight, yellows and golds, will deepen luck and attractiveness to others.

Virgo (August 24-September 23) Carnelian. The carnelian reflects the life force, and though life may take one from the heights to the depths (Virgo is a sign of extremes) this stone is warm and constant.

Libra (September 24-October 23) Jade, emerald. This is the sign of balance and harmony. Jade and emerald signify essential values – how does one define what is precious? When the soul is balanced against the weight of a feather at the gates of the afterlife, what will its value be? These beautiful stones hold the key to the answer.

Scorpio (October 24-November 22) Citrine. Intense and fanatical, the Scorpio subject is reminded to aim for a rational and steady outlook by the citrine stone. Softly glowing, warm without being burning hot, avoiding the intensity of rubies, garnets, sapphires, the citrine inspires all-round health and integration.

It is sometimes claimed that the opal, the stone of luck for October, is unlucky if worn by those whose birthday is in another month. In fact, the properties of the opal are to bring hidden emotions and repressed feelings to the surface. When such developments occur, the results can be difficult to deal with, as long-concealed resentments, loves, and other strong drives make themselves evident. Tensions, confrontations and similar awkward situations could well seem to be the result of the opal causing bad luck – but the tangles of life are not always easy to resolve, and when a stream is dammed up the rubbish must be cleared patiently away before the water can flow freely on in its appointed channel.

Sagittarius (November 23-December 21) Topaz. The gold of yellow topaz indicates eternal optimism, the constant striving of the Sagittarian mind to leap forward and reach higher things, on all planes, mental and physical. Let the topaz guide and inspire even when the flight of the arrow is fast or far.

Capricorn (December 22-January 20) Black diamond, jet. There is a great sense of tradition, of the proper way to go about things in the symbolism of jet and the formality of the black diamond. Everything proceeds in proper fashion, there is a right time and place, and you illustrate these precepts with stately dignity.

Aquarius (January 21-February 19) Quartz crystal. The mind of the Aquarian is as fluid as the luminous crystal, as clear and sparkling as water. Hold the idea and the moment as crystal does, frozen in an instant, before it flows on.

Pisces (February 20-March 20) Pearl, aquamarine. Aquamarine is one of the loveliest and rarest of stones, while pearl is not a stone, but a miracle gift from within the oyster's shell. Pisces is the highest aspiring sign of the zodiac, so allow these gems to emphasize your special qualities.

5. Let the past and its conflicts and fears go, feel at ease in the present. Spend time relaxing, being good to yourself physically. A Reiki healer advises that laying hands softly on the knees, or even gently massaging them, especially at the back, can be immensely soothing. Much of the trauma of our past is stored in the knees, causing tension and pain, even crippling.

6. Have water somewhere around you in the form of an indoor fountain or if this is not possible, relax to a tape of the sound of water. The Celts worshipped at sacred wells,

springs and streams. When undertaking spiritual journeys into the Otherworld, it was at these sources of water that the magic was most powerful and the way through was easiest to find.

7. Spell To Free You From Intimidation

If you feel intimidated, or even threatened, by the presence of another person, at work, perhaps, or living near you, obtain a photograph of the person or draw a picture roughly representing him or her. Mount the image on thin card, and carefully cut it into jigsaw pieces. At any time when you feel particularly vulnerable:

i. Burn a small amount of sage in a dish. The smoke cleanses and removes negative influence.

ii. Assemble the picture pieces and hold the image near the burning sage.

iii. Pronounce the following – *You have no power over me, it is drifting away with the smoke. I have no fear of you any more, because you are just made up of bits and pieces and they cannot hurt me.*

iv. Scatter the jigsaw pieces on the floor.

v. Repeat this ritual any time you feel the person in question threatens your peace of mind.

8. If You Want To Conceive

Apart from malfunction or serious medical conditions, the main problem which hinders conception is stress, tension, anxiety and other forms of worry. You need first of all to check with your doctor that there is no obvious reason why you cannot conceive, and then resolve to treat the matter with the seriousness it deserves. Do not make desperate or 'last ditch' attempts to become pregnant while holding down a highly demanding job, having a hectic social life, jetting to all parts of the globe. You are about to create life – this is a hallowed privilege and must be treated as such.

i. Arrange to take some time off with your partner – two weeks if possible.

ii. Choose somewhere that both of you consider sacred in some way – not necessarily in a religious way – and plan a pilgrimage together, on your own, to make your private prayer for the gift of life.

iii. Pinpoint the focus of your pilgrimage – a rock, a mountain, a lake or waterfall, a church, a shrine – and spend a little time there while you make your prayer.

iv. Having made your prayer, do not worry. Leave it with the higher power to whom you have made the request, and have faith. Share your return journey together and enjoy your closeness.

9. **To Ensure a Favourable Outcome at Litigation**
Write in black ink (not ball-pen or felt-tip) on a piece of parchment (not paper) the following talisman:

```
A L M A N A H
L
M A R E
A A L B E H A
N
A R E H A I L
H            A
```

Keep the talisman with you in order to persuade the judge in the case to view you and your concerns in a favourable light. This has its origin in a *grimoire* (book of magical secrets) which dates from 1458 and is known as the *Sacred Magic of Abra-Melin, the Mage*. It is known to have been used by such figures as Aleister Crowley, the 'Great Beast' who is widely regarded by those who know, as one of the most powerful magicians in recent times, in spite of his bizarre and erratic lifestyle.

Remember, however, that the principles of magic go deeper than the apparently obvious. One young woman to whom I gave this talisman, to use when her boyfriend was taken to court, reported that he had been given a substantial fine. 'But at least,' she added hopefully, 'he did not go to prison.'

Comparatively speaking, then, this was a favourable

result. Once again it is important to remember that magic does not somehow rub out all the difficult or awkward situations we may have to face in life. Such expectations are naïve and childish, and reflect the general belief that by consulting a 'witch' or secret practitioner in deep dark spells, we can have things sorted out for us without having to take the responsibility for the decisions and acts involved.

Much closer to our own time, this principle of avoiding responsibility and turning away, as it were, while someone else carries out the 'dirty work', found embodiment in the figure of the Sin Eater, who loomed large at funerals and, for a fee, publicly took upon himself the sins of the departed, leaving the dead soul free (it was assumed) to pass on to comfortable rest.

This practice was common along the Welsh borders, (a law unto themselves, and not strictly Celtic), and it is mentioned in *Precious Bane* by the Shropshire novelist Mary Webb.

10. **How to Maintain Your Balance in a Relationship**
This can be followed at all times, whether in a love relationship or not. It applies just as effectively to relationships within families.

i. Retreat to a quiet place where you can be private. If you have a room of your own and can shut everyone else out if you choose to be alone, all the better. If not, find a corner of the garden, or if you have to leave the place where you live in order to be alone in a public park, or some similar spot, do this.

ii. Sit quietly for a few moments, feeling your personal space around you, and then concentrate on a small box or container which you have ready. Tell yourself, as you look at the empty box: *Whatever I give to another of my own free will, or whatever is taken from me against my will, this box holds the essence of my self, and I vow that it will never pass from my possession. No-one and nothing will ever own me or possess me utterly and entirely. My self belongs to me. It was given to me freely when I was born and I will treasure it and care for it always.*

iii. Having made your affirmation, put into the box one by one a number of small, personal items that you have chosen to represent yourself to yourself. They do not need to be valuable, nor any kind of insurance against hard times. As you proceed in your life, you may choose to update them so that they are representative of the moment, rather than, say, of ten years before. The box must not be used as a weapon of defence or self-justification, or as an escape, but simply to remind you at times when you feel you have plunged too deeply into difficult emotional seas, or have lost your way, that you still exist as an individual. Remind yourself that whatever happens, your box empowers you to take control of your own life and future, whatever is happening in the present, or has happened in the past.

iv. Keep your box somewhere safe and private, and in times when your sense of identity is shaken, take it out in a quiet moment and recollect your affirmation, repeating it again as you touch and examine your links with your self. Do not share this experience with anyone, however deeply you love them. It is your own personal revelation and celebration of your self, something only you, as an individual, can appreciate. It comes from within, rather than from without, and will underline your personal strength, value and uniqueness.

11. **How to Achieve Youth and Beauty**
Youth and beauty have little to do with being young in years or possessing classical features. Both are states of mind. But here are a few practical hints to work the magic:

i. Go out and wash your face with dew as the dawn breaks on May Day. (The mere effort will do you the world of good.)

ii. Identify scents or perfumes which have confident, good-feeling associations in your past, and wear them rather than whatever is fashionable. It is no use drenching yourself in (say) Chanel No 5 if for some reason this classic always makes you personally feel tearful. Scents have immense power to evoke feelings – so leave heavy, oriental perfumes alone if you are aware that it is the simple flowery drift of cottage gardens in sunlight (for instance) that always gives you a great, got-your-act together lift.

iii. Communicate with nature. If you have a private garden, run out for a few minutes into torrential rain or a thunderstorm, wearing only a light robe – or nothing, if you dare – and drench yourself in the natural energy. When the moon is particularly clear, stand out-of-doors wearing nothing but your robe (or, in the Wiccan phraseology, strip right off and be 'sky-clad') and soak yourself in moonlight, opening yourself to it. Remember the moon is your link with the goddess – speak to her and let her speak to you.

iv. Hold a celebratory party at forty, at fifty, at sixty or whenever you like, not simply to remind yourself that 'life begins at ...' but to hymn yourself for your sheer physical success at reaching the age in question. There are so many disasters which might befall a human soul (and its body) on the journey through this life. The soul at forty, or at sixty, is still the same soul which struggled to take its first breath when it was born – indeed, will still be the same for as long as it remains alive. To have managed to survive comparatively safely, and to have done things, contributed to other people, progressed, is an incredible achievement. Give yourself credit for trying, for your successes in whatever fields, salute your soul for the wisdom it has accumulated and can use in the years to come. Reassure it that it has coped for fifty (sixty, seventy or whatever) years, and that it will cope just as effectively with whatever is to happen in the future with competence and dignity. Help it to feel good – growing older does not mean we should forget how to appreciate simple enjoyment in living.

v. Find something – a video, a cartoon, a book – which you know from experience will make you laugh, and keep it around so that you will be able to laugh regularly. Laugh often, smile every time you remember to. Instead of a drinks party, hold a laughter party, where the funniest outfit, the funniest face, the funniest joke, song, will help you to let go naturally, and release tension. For a wonderful sex life, just try *laughing* together.

From the Goddess:
Meditation on Beauty

There is no element of beauty in existence, there is only the exquisite harmony of pure balance. For each object has a counterpart and each light a contrasting shadow to comprise the whole. And yet there is beauty such that the breath will catch in the throat and the heart will swell so that the agony of beholding such loveliness is beyond bearing.

Aspire to such beauty, for it is a seed within, which will flower in the right season and when it is worshipfully cultivated.

A woman longs to be beautiful. She comes to the goddess in the light of the waning moon with a sacrifice in her hand, the cockerel struggling pitifully. The way to my altar is barred to her. I am not concerned with the dark which seeks to pass itself off as the light.

Another hides her face from her lover, yet when he turns it towards him, the radiance is like the starry beauty of the Pleiades, and he weeps, dazzled with wonder.

12. A Ritual For Confidence

As we go through the day, we are assaulted on all sides by other people's negativity. You may find you always come out of an encounter with a particular shop assistant, colleague or neighbour feeling upset and shaky for no reason. The more psychic ability you possess (and everyone has some) the more you will be affected. To avoid this, it is necessary to protect yourself by surrounding yourself with positivity before any such encounters arise.

Imagine you are standing beneath a huge tin of white paint, and that it is tipping up, drenching every part of you so that you are covered in white. Think of the white as positivity, buoyance, and tell yourself that anyone throwing negative energy towards you will feel it bounce back from your lovely positive protective shield.

You can also use the image of stepping into a white suit like those used to protect the wearer against radiation. Step in, feel your protective suit close round your arms, glove your fingers, stretch a helmet over your head through which you can see. You do not need to *do* anything to protect yourself. Leave it to the positivity, the Light, and let tension and apprehension go in the awareness that the defences around you are too powerful for any malicious spite or selfish preoccupation to penetrate.

It is for protection also that symbols such as the Cross, Star of David, Eye of Horus (or even, if such a token were available at a jeweller's, Head of Bendigeid Vran) are worn. Wear whatever you think will help protect you against the negativity in the world around you, whether a gem stone or a symbol of faith. Turquoise protects, and is traditionally used for this purpose in many parts of the world, from the 'blue bead' popular in the East to decorate a car or a camel, to the silver ornaments of native Indians in both North and South America, which are studded with turquoise.

13. Freeing Yourself From a Distressing Incident

When something upsetting happens, you may, in your distress, view it out of all proportion to its actual importance in your life. Incidents where you feel you have made a fool of yourself, said or done something unforgivable, destroyed your credibility or created a dreadful impression, can seriously undermine your feelings of self-worth, and because of this, you may blunder into further situations, losing more and more of your confidence each time.

Whatever the incident, take the following action when you have the opportunity to spend a few moments quietly on your own.

i. Sit down with a watch or clock in your hand, and set it to just before the time the upsetting incident happened.

102

Speak aloud and tell yourself: *I am returning to three o'clock this afternoon* (or whatever the time was). *This was the time of my interview* (or whatever the incident was).

ii. Tell yourself that it does not matter what actually happened. You have been given an opportunity to return and correct what went wrong.

iii. In your mind, run through what happened at the incident as though it was a film. But this time, remember that – though you were too distressed, embarrassed or upset to realize it at the time – *you were the star*. Once you perceive that you yourself played the most important role, everyone else was actually a supporting character, you will be able to appreciate all the actions you took which you can applaud. Those little omissions (like forgetting to say thank you, or failing to give someone else credit) can be easily put right in a minute, and without any need to create a scene. There is nothing which could possibly have taken place that need really matter to you, or damage your good feelings about yourself and your future.

If you were really upset or hurt, and find it difficult to forget what happened, concentrate again on all the star qualities you displayed. You may have kept your temper under great provocation, overcome your personal fears or phobias, or shown unexpected courage. Even if you did give way, you can be quite sure you had good reason, and rather than upset yourself, concentrate on the fact that you have a right to feel anger and a right to insist that your needs must be properly met.

Anger, kept down, while the personality carries a burden of shame, guilt and a sensation that 'it was really all my fault' can cripple you for life, so do remember that, as *the star* in the unfolding story of your life, you have a right to be fair to yourself, at the very least. Give yourself the benefit of the doubt, praise yourself rather than blame.

No one can do more than their best. You need never feel that your best is unacceptable, but your potential may be far greater than you think

For All who Want Love – From the Goddess

Wrap yourself in your cloak and go forward fearlessly towards love, and it will come towards you with hands outstretched. Demand love like a fretful child and it will turn its face from you.

For there is only one way to receive love and that is to give it. Even the most humble who kneel at the altar of the goddess ask for nothing, but offer themselves, living jewels, at my feet. Upon them I pour the sacred oil of my blessing. They go forth into the world and love shines from them like the soft glow of a lamp and brings light into the dark corners where the frightened souls cower.

And love dwells in the crystal fountain that splashes in the courtyard where the oleanders bloom, and where the shadows of desire fall ever longer across the mosaic floor. A nightingale waits with liquid in its throat to throw its droplets of silver into the blue of the night sky. Starry burn the fires of love, and the silver maiden with tresses of silver and opal stars within her eyes is merged into the silver body of the warrior, and the two become one. And in the pool, the small stars that have fallen from the heavens lie like jewels.

And the two spirits sink slowly to rest upon the pillow of the heavens, and their love binds them with cords of silver overlaid with gold. The warrior and the maiden will drift for ever among the planets and rival the shooting stars for brightness.

And I charge you to love most of all the spirit that is within you. Stoke up the beacon of your self with love until it burns high and clear, and walk the dim corridors of your life with this torch held in your hand so that the red flames may illumine them. Tenderly care for your own spirit, for it is alone in an alien place and in its vulnerability it is to you that it must turn.

Nurture your spirit and love it with complete acceptance of its flaws, for the unsullied, the untouched and perfect have no place in the struggle for growth. Carry your scars like battle flags and display them proudly, and honour your spirit for its victories. This is the word of the goddess. Until you can unreservedly love yourself you have nothing to give to another.

And yet without love there is no hope for the soul. It rises like the lark in the morning, higher and higher into the blue sky, carry-

ing in its beak the thread of gold that will shower the weeping heart with softest balm, and the agonized with the petals of peace. This is the word of the goddess. Love and be loved, for this is the only way along which the human soul can pass to reach its destination.

The Language of Magic

iii

Colours There are various methods of using colour beneficially, choosing colours to reveal your hidden self, finding the colours which suit you so far as everyday living and the dictates of fashion go. These are often not at all what you expect – for instance, I was amazed to find when given such a test, that a boring colour I did not even like much, Prussian blue, changed my reflection as though by magic into something stunningly attractive and alive, leaving the vibrant reds and greens as 'also rans'.

Colours themselves are illusions, and do not really exist. Both black and white are extremes of the spectrum, and contain all the colours in between. Yet the movement and variation of light which form colours are accompanied by similar changes in the aura, the electro-magnetic (energy) field that, as we have seen, surrounds all life forms. And such changes we might truthfully describe as 'the nuances of the voice of God' (or the Goddess).

From the Goddess
On Beauty
The colours of beauty are many, and may not always be found within the spectrum. So lovely are certain of these colours that they are of necessity never revealed upon the earth as they would shatter the human eye as a careless pebble might shatter the glass which holds the vision within its pool of light.

Yet there have been vouchsafed glimpses of these colours. Close your eyes to your surroundings and within the sanctuary of the

glade of the goddess, reach with the deepest yearnings of your
spirit for beauty. Beneath my protection, you will find the way,
and, if you are worthy, be vouchsafed the awareness.

Traditionally, the colours of the spectrum possess their own
meaning. Red vibrates with passion and energy; blue is
cool; green is restful; black is withdrawn and isolated.
Investigate the colours which will heal you physically,
mentally and spiritually. Learn with the help of a good
reference work (see reading list) to be able to view the
colours of the aura for yourself. I was highly flattered
when, early on in my psychic and spiritual development, I
asked a very experienced fellow clairvoyant what colour
my own aura was, and he considered through half-closed
eyes. Then:

'Antique gold,' he pronounced without hesitation,
explaining when I enquired what it meant, that it signified
'ancient wisdom'. I thought this the loveliest compliment I
have ever been paid.

Numerology The magic of numbers is ancient and powerful. The practice of numerology links numbers with the
letters of the alphabet (various different alphabets, actually)
and can be used for divination and as a way of 'seeing
clear'.

A numerologist might begin by calculating your 'root'
number, using the letters of your name and his chosen
system of numbers – based on the Hebrew alphabet, for
example. In my own case, my name would be set out as
follows:

D I L Y S   G A T E R
4 13 13 3   3 1 4 5 2

The numbers are added together – in my case, they make
a total of 27. But except in certain cases, double figures are
added together to make a single one – in my case, the

number 9.

Referring to interpretive data, or his own knowledge, the numerologist can cast light via the number 9 on my personality and the way I have tackled my life. As a 9, I am a charming, passionate high achiever, someone who inspires and cares for others, but insists on doing it in my own way. The 'heart' number and 'birth' number (using the subject's date of birth) can begin to reveal the faces you present to the world, your private, hidden self, and taken even further, the calculations of the numerologist will advise on how to conduct yourself in the future, or ways in which you might help to make your path easier. For instance, if the letters of your name clash (numerologically speaking) with other findings about you, based on your birth date, say, you could take the beneficial step of changing your name so that your numbers were more harmonious. It is well known that the British royal family changed its name to Windsor – but was this entirely to avoid a foreign sounding word? And was 'Windsor' simply a random choice? Just consider the following numerological information: the numerical values of the letters run like this:

$$\begin{array}{ccccccc} W & I & N & D & S & O & R \\ 6 & 1 & 5 & 4 & 3 & 7 & 2 \end{array}$$

Perfect balance is achieved here since every number from 1 to 7 is included. The total is 28, which adds up to 10, which counts as 1. And the main properties of the number 1 are power and singlemindedness. Not always likeable, 1s find loving relations difficult, and are inclined to be domineering. The numbers 8 and 9 (representing material success and great spiritual achievement) are left out – but they are not all-important to a royal dynasty.

In contrast to this well-balanced, stable, egocentric but slightly dull image – the sort of thing that would inspire confidence in a nervous public – the previous family name adds up to 5. This is the number of dark sexual activity, irresponsibility, gambling and risks

(See reading list for reference works on Numerology).

Sacred Magic of Abra-Melin, The Mage Each magician, wise man or wise woman works in their own personal way, drawing up their own spells, as their own powers dictate. When consulting any book to find a spell, one should remember that talismans, charms, and other magical formulae are rarely at their most effective unless the intent – the will, the belief, whatever you call it – is added. Each person therefore creates his or her own magic according to the intensity of personal energy they put into it.

6

The Goddess, The Search, The Grail

Prepare the altar and light the flame, for I am come. Though there be no gatherers in my name, yet still from the glaciers of the north and the waterfalls of the south I will come, though the time be long and the waiting wearisome. Though there is no shadow to greet me, yet I am come, and because of my presence, the small creatures in the forest relax their vigilance and sleep, and the hunted deer rests her weariness and the trapped resign their souls and die.

I am the passion that runs through the book of days which makes up a sojourn upon the earth, the sap in the stem and the blood pulsing through the heart, blue and gold, illuminated by the ponderous pen of an aged monk, and the light of the eye, the fleetness of the foot of youth, the pain which pierces deeper than nails into the palms of the emaciated Christ, the wonder that cannot be contained within the cupped hands of the spring child at the fountain.

The Goddess

When mention is made of the Goddess, the most common reaction is: 'Which goddess do you mean?' or 'Who is she?'

It is only with a background like that of Christianity, with a monotheistic male deity, that one has to question the appearance of *the* Goddess (or even *a* goddess), but some souls intuitively know of her and feel at one with her.

John, a laid-back personality of few words, contacted me for a reading which was conducted on the phone. He was tough and unsentimental. After we had dealt with more general matters of his difficulty in getting a job, loneliness and lack of close friends – the usual problems of mid-life today – it became apparent that there was something deeper worrying him, and eventually he must have felt he could trust me enough to air his problem. Without any explanation of the details, he said simply:

'I desperately need to worship the Goddess. I have been told by other psychics and mediums not to do it, but trying to do without her in my life is making me ill. I suppose you will say the same, but I cannot go on without her any longer.'

My immediate reaction was of irritation at such short-sightedness, since the man was patently suffering from intense inner conflict and frustration. His very genuine attempts at enlightenment seemed to have been dismissed in the most cursory way.

'Why should I tell you not to worship the Goddess?' I asked him. 'I am intensely aware of her loveliness and power, and I act for her, as it were. If you feel such a strong need to worship her, I think she might very well fill the yawning gap you were telling me about (he had no close female friend or lover). She will provide you with the focus for your devotion and your chivalry that you so badly want.'

His voice changed. He seemed amazed – disarmed.

'You think it would be all right? I have tried so many people, and they all put me off. I have been getting desperate to find permission to worship her.'

'You are a mature man, you do not need my permission or anyone else's to put your faith in any god – or goddess,' I said. 'I cannot understand why the other people you consulted have been so bigoted – I imagine they are not

110

very well informed about the Goddess, and what she stands for. I can see no reason why you should not go right ahead, you are free to go to her as soon as you put the phone down if you like, and make her a focal point of your everyday life – so long of course as your forms of worship are not harmful or upsetting to yourself or anyone else.'

This caution is necessary because solitary goddess-worshippers, especially men, often choose odd or sexually bizarre forms of expressing their devotion – as indeed solitary worshippers in other belief systems may also be inclined to do.

John sounded as though he had been given a reprieve from jail.

'I can't tell you how I feel, what a relief it is – to be able to acknowledge my faith openly—'

'As the knights of old pledged themselves to go forth in the name of their lady, you will go forward in the name of the Goddess, and know that you are her warrior. It is obvious from what I see that this is no passing thing. You do not really want to marry or get a girl-friend. You want to know you are a servant of the Goddess herself, that she is with you – as she will be – and that the light of your life comes from your devotion to her.'

John did not answer for a moment, then he said quietly:

'I did not realize – only the terrible need – but you are quite right, absolutely right, and now that I know, I feel as though a great burden has been lifted. Ecstatic, really. Wonderful. Thank you, thank you.'

'It won't be an easy life,' I warned him, and he swept that to one side.

'How can it be worse than being without her, cut off?'

Simply, the Goddess is the feminine aspect of the male image of God: the Supreme Being which has many names and many forms, according to the religion or belief from which you view him. All religions have their own names for the God-figure, the Creator, the Divine Being, the

Mother-Father, the Light, the Spirit. The god has been represented over the centuries as Baal, Jehovah, Osiris, Buddha, Quetzalcoatl – to name just a few. (Many of these names are simply titles meaning 'Father', 'Leader' or something similarly evocative and vague.) In essence, these are all the same god, and the different religions act as paths along which the faithful may pass in order to reach him.

The Goddess has had a more chequered history. In early civilizations, the female aspect of the god was often considered of more importance than the male, and the goddesses Astarte and Ashtoreth were just two who had their own cults. They were fierce and vengeful (similar to the Celtic Andrasta whom we have already encountered), often demanding human sacrifice – it was an early illustration of the precept that 'the female of the species is deadlier than the male', though Baal too devoured new-born infants and was worshipped by a devoted High Priestess in the form of the Biblical Jezebel.

More often than not, many gods and goddesses were active at the same time; Romans were shocked, for instance, when they learned that the new religion of the Christ had only one god – was it too poor, they wondered, to afford others? And each civilization had its own pantheon of gods and goddesses. Often one would become integrated into, or adopted by, the next. Both the Romans and the Christian church skilfully carried the hierarchy of Celtic deities a step further from the original. And in the east and west, the same gods and goddesses were differentiated only by different names.

As the centuries progressed, the qualities of strength and leadership came to be regarded as a masculine prerogative – outwardly, at any rate – and the feminine aspect of the god head became subservient to the power of the god, and later almost non-existent. The feminine, or 'goddess' aspect continued to run strongly underground, however, and even in Christianity the adoration of the feminine found expression in the worship of the Virgin Mary.

Within recent years, when there is more public tolerance involved in the whole attitude to worship, efforts have been made (particularly by some feminist groups, who take the view that because she is female, the Goddess is *ipso facto*, superior to any male gods), to revive the goddess cult. New importance has been placed on the worship of the Earth Mother and her relevance to our culture today. But what such misguided, though well-meaning people do not realize is that the Goddess does not need reviving. She has been with us all the time, and has never left.

Knight in Check

This symbolic text was channelled through from the Goddess; the title above is one I have given to it. It seems to me to represent on many levels the search undertaken by the soul to find answers, awareness, which though common to humanity as a whole, are nevertheless very personal to each individual. In a Celtic sense, the journey is one that is recognizable – through snows, forests, the horrors of death, returning at last, saved from extinction in fear, to rebirth, fresh wisdom, the coming of spring, the whole cycle which ruled the Celtic existence. Even more interesting is the secondary cycle illustrated here, which is revealed to the knight at the end – it is that of the phases of the moon (symbolizing the Goddess), appearing to threaten him with annihilation as the moon passes through its dark phase. In due course, when the moon becomes visible again, he is aware of the presence not only of the Goddess but of all that he had thought lost for ever.

There is here a vivid introduction not only to the Celtic goddess in her many aspects, 'awful' as well as beautiful, but also to a deeper investigation into the heart of Celtic belief, the journey made by the soul into dark and dangerous realms to find the Sacred Treasures of existence.

I sought her through the frozen forest, where the ground rang like iron, and across the icy stream, stilled in an eternity of perpetual time; I earnestly strove for her cloak, for her hood, covering the shape of her I loved and the fall of her hair. Without the sight of her I loved, the earth turned to ashes smouldering in the aftermath of a great Armageddon, and the sky was void for the moon had gone and the sun had burned itself out.

O, weary, weary the path where the fronds of dead fern were etched with crystal rime and the patches of water stood like pools of heaviness. With her she took the sweetness of the wild flowers, the poppy's blaze and the tiny stars of the gentian, the sunlight within the petals of primrose and the snow of the daisy. Without such things I cannot live, not to carry forth my armour and do battle with the giants and the demons who ride the passes of the mountains and overcome the unwary traveller. Without the gladness of the air which moves about her, so that she carries spring in her eyes and the caress of the sea wave and water in the desert within her touch, the grey ash and the arid sands will stop up my mouth and choke the breath from my lungs and the vultures will circle to pluck out my eyes as my soul perishes in the depths of Gehenna, where the smoke from the burning corpses never ceases and it is perpetual night.

I sought her in the depths of the forest, where the great unseen beasts lurked beyond the flame of my meagre fire, and the tall trees touched skies I could not see, and the snow fell constantly with no sound. Time had ceased, for the clock, even the sand-timer and the water-clock and the dial to catch the rays of the sun, had stopped, since time is propelled onwards by love, and all the love had gone.

I cried aloud to the Goddess not to leave me, I cried aloud to her to return, to start my heart once more and unfreeze the weight of tears which held me imprisoned, like a great stone within my breast. My cries echoed round the still, empty peaks of the desolate mountains, and returned to me, unfulfilled.

Without her the small creatures lay dying, the hare and the fieldmouse, the squirrel and the blue-coated mole, and there appeared great cracks in the frozen earth, and the very air froze. And then the dark fell on the crying and the whimpering and the suffering and the piteous small souls struggling to survive. And upon me, light as a cobweb or the touch of the wing of a butterfly, feathery with dust, came a great peace. And I opened my eyes and saw that the tip of the moon was there, zodiacal in the heavens, and beside me knelt the one I loved, her cloak spread round her feet, and there was sweet water at my mouth and pools of living light within her eyes. And the sands stirred in the hour-glass, and the water-clock began to drip, and the dial prepared itself once more for the sun.

Into Another Kingdom

The myths and tales of Celtic tradition contain incredible richness and power, love, hate, rivalry, magic which seems to be far beyond the intensities we experience today. They are larger than life, they concern passionate dedication to single-minded objectives, for the sake of which the protagonists will willingly fight to the death.

Many of these ancient tales are of journeys, and their true meanings are shadowy, but they symbolize the spiritual journeying of the soul, and its attempts to find the secrets of existence, which the Celts identified as objects of 'Holy or Precious Treasure'. The divine antiquity and the might from which these treasures emerged is also present in the form taken by the Tarot cards, whose history is shrouded in mist as far back as Ancient Mesopotamia.

The Tarot pack consists of seventy-eight cards, twenty-two of which make up the Major Arcana (the powerful picture cards) while fifty-six form the four suits in the Minor Arcana – swords, wands, cups and pentacles. The four treasures of Celtic spirituality are actually a sword, spear (wand), cauldron (cup) and stone (marker, representative of magic and wisdom, similar in its nature to a pentacle).

There is great depth to the Holy Treasures. Traditionally, four of them were brought to the world (or, in Irish myth, to Ireland) by the divine Tuatha de Danaan, the people of

115

the gods of Dana, or as some called them, the Men of Dea. Dana herself was one of the mother figures of Celtic belief. In the list of great goddesses (including Brigit) we are given the following in the translation by Lady Gregory: *'...there were many shadow-forms and great queens; but Dana, that was called the Mother of Gods, was beyond them all.'*

The Tuatha de Danaan arrived in a mist from their Otherworld cities. Since the Otherworld covers all the planes, planets or alternative existences beyond our awareness, it seems that this, like the cryptic writings in the Books of Isaiah and Ezekiel in the Old Testament (which have been interpreted as descriptions of visits by alien beings in some form of spacecraft) could be one more mysterious hint that there might indeed have been invasions of this planet from distant places where civilizations of great wisdom and enlightenment had established an apparent Utopia of peace.

We know the names of the four cities from which the Treasures came – *'great Falais, and shining Gorias, and Finias, and rich Murias that lay to the south'*. We are given the names of the four Wise Men who had tutored the Children of Dana in *'skill and knowledge and perfect wisdom'*. And Lady Gregory's description of the Treasures themselves shimmers with mysterious power.

'...a Stone of Virtue from Falais, that was called the Lia Fail, the Stone of Destiny; and from Gorias they brought a Sword; and from Finias a Spear of Victory; and from Murias the fourth treasure, the Cauldron that no company ever went away from unsatisfied.'

The tales in Celtic lore concerning the Treasures represent them as being often sought in long, fearful struggles in dark and dangerous circumstances by the heroes who would eventually bring them into the light. Basically speaking, this can be psychologically interpreted as symbolizing the struggle for self-awareness in the depths of the personality – but since such stories can be read on many levels, they give to each individual just what that person can deal with at any given time. On the level of pure story-telling, they make thrilling and racy reading. The Celts were far ahead of today's tabloids, being perhaps among the first to realize (superficially speaking, of course) that what their readers really wanted was sex and violence. As with most race myths, their tales were filled with both. And since they were mentally unencumbered by the embarrassment of concepts such as guilt and shame, they can seem frightening to nineties man and woman. But if we cannot accept their pagan way of thinking, we can at least appreciate the richness and brilliance of their tales, their symbolism and imagery. And we can share their Treasures.

The Holy Treasures of the Gods

The four Holy Treasures of the Tuatha de Danaan, as we have seen, were a Sword, a Spear, a Cauldron and a Stone. But each was incredible, magical, powerful, a symbol that stood for all that was wise and sacred and enduring in human understanding. When you are dealing with gods, however, the wise, sacred and enduring may not always be easy or pleasant, they do not simply scratch the surface of living, but go deep to the dark and tangled roots of existence, and are often only attained after bitter struggle.

It is sometimes claimed that belief systems which seem to make a virtue out of suffering have the wrong idea, and in these days when a new millennium is beginning, perhaps we need to consider this matter seriously. For there is too much suffering in the world – in fact, the whole of history, viewed realistically and from a detached perspective, shows us that there has always been too much suffering. It comes to the attention of the human race in waves – sometimes the absorption is with the victims of war, sometimes it shifts to the plight of children, or animals, or of those with a particular type of illness. But it never stops, and try as we may, we find it the most difficult of realities to cope with.

Why does it happen? What is the meaning of it all? What can we do about it?

The Celts, as pagans, do not provide – or even attempt to provide – bland, 'summing it all up easily' answers, and their beliefs, which incorporate acceptance of seeming cruelty and unnecessary sacrifice and suffering, can strike a note of alarm in a modern mind. The Goddess herself reveals that she does not flinch from the dark and dreadful side of nature (including human nature) and views both the object and its shadow dispassionately and with no trace of sentimentality.

The ability to accept, to look reality in the face and not flinch or try to pretend it is 'all right', reflects the theories of the most spiritual of the great psychological theorists, C.G. Jung. It was he who formulated the concept of the *shadow* – the dark part of the self which we do not want to acknowledge. In the *shadow*, all the fears and failings we cannot face or cope with, find their home.

But even though we do not want to recognize them, they still exist. It is necessary for cosmic balance, for perfect symmetry and harmony, that the dark and the light, like the Yin-Yang, the absolutes of Good and Evil, are not only acknowledged, but accepted as parts of the whole. It is the dynamics of the on-going struggle between them that creates the ideal, rather than the complete wiping out of one or the other. And just as the polarities must exist to balance each other, the 'flat line' of utter mediocrity is meaningless. Without the depths, how can there be an appreciation of the peaks of existence? Without an acquaintanceship with the rotten, how can there be an awareness of blessings that promise hope and new birth, gifts that are fresh and new?

The Celts did accept. They knew and acknowledged the cycle of life, which began with dark death and wanderings in the Underworld, where the fearsome king Arawn kept his state. In all nature, the stirrings of birth followed, the growing, the flowering, the ripening, the inevitable drawing in of the life-span as decay and darkness set in once more. Even the goddesses of Celtic belief are similarly complex, and bear, in a great many cases, a triple face, that of the ancient Wise Crone, the Maiden of spring loveliness, and the all-nurturing Mother or Lady.

The Celtic cycle did not begin with inexperience and birth, it began with death, darkness and ancient wisdom, returning after life to the dark kingdom once more.

Strangely, however, the traditional Celtic heaven is represented as the Tir na Nog, the Land of Eternal Youth, where the soul never ages, but remains for ever young and beautiful. Perhaps that is the reward earned by those who pass through the journey of life and acquit themselves with the courage and heroism that was the attribute of those heroes of myth. For they too passed through the journey of life, and fought to arm and save themselves and those who depended upon them with the Holy Treasures of the Gods – which, veiled in mystic meaning, can arm and save us in a similar way today.

The Sword of Light

This belonged to Nuada, king of the Children of Dana. He represents a form of human adjustment to us because he lost an arm in battle with the Firbolgs, the so-called 'Men of the Bag' who occupied Ireland when the Children of Dana arrived. Thus flawed (the king must be perfect) he eventually gave his place to the god Lugh, variously described as Lugh Lamh Fada (Lugh of the Long Arm) and Lugh Ildanach (the Consummate Craftsman). Nuada was fitted with a silver arm (every finger moveable) to replace the one he had lost by a great healer of the Tuath, and is known as Nuada Argentlam (Nuada of the Silver Hand).

The sword took the form in later stories of King Arthur's mystic sword Excalibur, and another of the Treasures, the Cauldron, became the embodiment of that dream of all perfect desires, the Holy Grail. In pagan tradition, the Grail

119

was the Cauldron of the Dagda, a never-ceasing source of food and refreshment for both mind and body – in Christian belief, the Grail was the actual Cup from which Jesus had drunk wine at the Last Supper, the one he had offered to his disciples with the words: 'This is my blood'. The one thing which is certain is that, in spite of all the stories and legends, the solemn quests and journeys undertaken by the Knights of Arthur's Round Table, neither the Cauldron nor the Grail were ever found, except in dreams and visions.

For although they were real things in the ancient accounts, none of the Treasures was tangibly real at all. The Sword represents the power not of physical force, but of the mind, of spiritual energy which can create order from chaos. Significantly, Nuada is noted as a Celtic deity of water, of healing and therapy, and of the mystery and significance of the position of a king – in early Celtic times far more vital than it is today, and deeply associated in an almost divine form with the kingdom itself.

The Spear of Lugh

The spear traditionally carried victory with it. Lugh was one of the greatest of that divine race of Dana, perhaps the most notable god of the Celts. He was the embodiment of light and fire, and it is said that to the Celts the darting of summer lightning marked the god's passing, and the hissing and snapping of his spear. The spear represents the indomitable energy of the power of the will and what it can accomplish. With this weapon, we can overcome bodily weakness and fear, adverse circumstances and all that the rest of the world can hold against us. However, apart from his skill with the spear and also the slingshot, Lugh was known to be a craftsman, artisan, and generally so gifted that there was nothing he could not do brilliantly – this perhaps illustrates that the prudent soul sets its mind on its goal, but makes sure that practical necessities are attended to as well.

The Cauldron of the Dagda

The Dagda was the greatest of the Irish gods, a father figure in more ways than one. He was the God of Wisdom as well as the Great Father, but for some reason was often represented as a sort of Falstaffian character, who lumbered round in clothes so short that his buttocks were visible, eating and drinking gigantically, and with a permanent eye on the women. Tales of his sexual prowess are dramatically detailed, and include ribald – sometimes terrifying – encounters not only with human partners, but with goddesses whose power rivalled his own, including the dread Morrigan, the violent triple-faced goddess of sexuality and death.

The never-emptying Cauldron of the Dagda reflects the simple summing-up of the needs of life – food for the body and the ability to procreate; food for the soul, emotional fulfilment, increasing growth and knowledge.

I have found examples many times in my work that people who have problems continue to find – and lose – the answers which will help them. When they are given a suggested course of behaviour, or explanation of patterns which have occurred in their lives, they will say: 'Yes, that makes sense, it explains everything. Yes, I see it all now.' And yet I know that almost everybody in such a situation will find it recurs over and over, the answer, when unearthed once again, always seeming as though it is being given for the first time. It is as though we are born with perfect knowledge, but we are unable to keep track of all of it, and so have to manage on a fraction of that wisdom and awareness, changing our grip on it from time to time. In actual fact, all spiritual wisdom is the same, and it is extremely simple, something one *is* rather than learns.

Perhaps the dramatic sexuality of the all-embracing Dagda and his eternal Cauldron are there to provide us with hope. The sources of life, procreation, emotion, imagination, growth, knowledge and wisdom are always there. Nature never dries up or decides she has given enough – the bird does not protest that it has sung more than its fair share, or the water refuse to flow because it is negotiating a pay-rise. Each day is as beautiful as the one before. We must accept the facts the Ancient Crone reveals to us – the dark does come, and the journey down into the twilit kingdom of Annwn. But in the meantime, we can choose between a state of 'lacking', where we feel a constant need to compensate ourselves and lay up stocks against the disasters we fear will come, or a celebration of 'abundance', as we regard our blessings and the treasures we have been freely given, with the faith that the source of such gifts will not fail us. This is, very simply, a choice between positive and negative thinking, between optimism and pessimism. We may well find that nothing changes materially, but how much more pleasant if we are determined to see the best in everything and enjoy what we have.

The Stone of Destiny

This was set up in the kingdom of Tara, to preside over the coronation of the rightful kings of Erin, the Ard Righ. When a rightful king was crowned, the stone pronounced its approval with a shattering roar, making it clear that the ceremonies were proceeding in a proper manner.

It is this sense of truth, of rightfulness, that we can apply to our own lives today, because as with a kingdom, if the central figure, the king, is worthy, then that worth will be reflected as far as the furthest boundaries. If we base our lives on our own truths, setting standards and keeping to whatever we see as right, that sense of rightness will radiate from us, however 'ordinary' our lives may seem. We will be fulfilling our own destinies, our own appointed places in the great scheme of things.

The Face of the Goddess

It may seem confusing when one speaks of 'the goddess' to describe her at the same time as 'triple-aspected' or 'three-faced', 'the Ancient Crone, the Maiden and the Mother'. A comparison with the Anglican God who is yet 'Father, Son and Holy Ghost' will illustrate how the idea works.

Descriptions of the goddess are gleaned from ancient tales and myths, recorded by later generations, and from archaeological evidence in the form of carvings and inscriptions. The goddess herself is a presence, a power to be invoked in whichever form we choose to see her, or in whichever form she chooses to appear. But different goddesses are recognizable by their own special attributes – though as they may 'shape-shift' they may be seen in many other forms besides.

The goddess Sirona – mentioned earlier as the source of the channelled material in this book – was represented both in her own right, and as the consort of Apollo Grannus, the Celtic Apollo, god of healing. Her name is derived from the word for star, but she also appears as the Mother, or Lady, holding a little dog in her arms. Her powers are symbolized by her ornaments – upon her hair a diadem signifies her high state and power, while a snake is clasped round her arm, its head pointing towards the hand, which carries three eggs that signify fertility.

There were shrines to Sirona (and her consort) throughout the ancient areas of Europe and beyond. She was a water goddess, her shrines flowing with healing springs, and her power as a dispenser of healing as well as of fertility was ancient long before the Roman legions trod the shores of Britain.

In her own words, these are the images she gives of herself:

I am the goddess of the silver spring, who led the unicorn by a thread of crimson safely through the tangled thickets of the forest and before whom the giant babe-eater Behemoth, foaming blood as he gnashed his teeth and screamed his misery to the stars, hiding their sacred fires, knelt to kiss the tip of my robe. Prostrate he lay, and from the black hole of his mouth streamed the black slime of the knowledge of evil and upon the surface of the water near alighted a white swan, to fade like a wraith of loveliness into the dusk, and the night darkened.

I am fire and shadow, the flame and the darker flame that surrounds it, I am the red cloud of the outer flame and the fierce intensity of the inner core, I am the dancing floor on which the measure is beaten out and the feet which dance, the hands on the drumskins and the sounds they make, the white body of the woman like a lily placed in homage and the body of the man another to lie beside it on a bed of moss, within the tangled webs of her rainbow hair.

7

Interpreter of Wisdom

It is difficult to have confidence in your own ability to find
the truth, but it is even more difficult to have confidence in
the ability of others to find it for you. Ultimately you tread
that narrow road alone. Truth is an experience you must
live through for yourself.

Yvaine Huath

Before enlightenment
chopping wood
carrying water.

After enlightenment
chopping wood
carrying water.

Zen proverb

Whatever wisdom the past gives to us, we need to harness
it to the present, so that we can go forward to seek and
benefit from the wisdom of the future. Many sitters have
told me after a reading (as no doubt other seekers have told
their own personal advisers) that: 'You have helped me to
see clearly what I really knew all the time.' In reality, everyone knows all the answers they need – but it is often difficult to perceive the truth. The task of the wise woman is
therefore not to tell others what to do, or to do it for them,
but to help them find the strength and ability to cope in
their own right and in their own way.

What exactly is wisdom, and what makes any person

wise? What does the Wise Woman possess that gives her the authority to speak? In my experience it has nothing to do with extra knowledge, it is not an additional store of facts or that she can claim to 'know better' than others. Rather it is a mental state, an ability to connect with many different sources of wisdom and apply them to the problems of living.

In my case, the connections have often been literal. I have been given the ability to open my mind to sources in the past and in the distant planes of existence, I have been able to perceive and record wisdom and messages of many kinds, some of which I have shared with you in this book. When I feel impelled to do so, I can connect, as easily as making a telephone call, with other spiritual planes, and other intellects, and whether the messages actually come from my own Higher Self, or from mystical enlightenment by angels, aliens or even sheer delusion, does not seem to me to be worth arguing about. For the one thing that is certain about them is that they will stand up in their own right to critical scrutiny. They are filled with many depths of infinite wisdom which are entirely their own.

I have sometimes found it difficult to explain to enquirers exactly how the intuitive channelling process happens, or indeed, why I personally, rather than a member of the Royal Family or Joe Brown in Huddersfield, should be the one to receive messages from Outer Space. Regarding this second point, I am by no means the only person who can channel, and in fact, we will be examining in the second part of this chapter how literally *anyone* can make a start at opening mental communications with different sources of wisdom and intelligence.

The actual process varies with each individual, and since nobody else has ever explained clearly to me what their particular method is, I can only speak for myself. It would perhaps be wise to do this now.

Opening the Doors

It is impossible to mistake channelling or messages from outside yourself for anything else, if you follow your intuition and are scrupulously honest with yourself. If you show what you have written to other people, you may fear that doubts will be placed on your sanity, or that they may laugh, but – as so often on the spiritual path – the truth, once revealed, speaks for itself.

The process itself does no harm, except that it uses up energy. Probably for this reason, I have found that it is almost impossible to 'channel' constantly over long periods of time, and if you try to do this, you will probably block whatever communications you might have made by over-anxiety, and – once again, the real barrier to spiritual progress – by letting your brain and your logic get in the way. The spur that prompts me to actually sit down and open my mind seems to be *need* – and if, as was the case with the goddess texts, they seem to arrive without being asked for, there appears to have been an underlying need for the information which I might not have been aware of.

The process involves simply sitting down quietly, protecting yourself as outlined earlier with a simple prayer, resolving to open your mind to any messages or communications that come, and then doing just that. When open to information – from any source – I personally do not hear voices, but I can sense the communicating intellect flipping through what is stored in my own mind, so that it can frame sentences and find the right words, as though my brain were a computer. This happens at an incredible speed, telepathically, which can mean that all the information is given to me at once, and it is only the need to find a framework by means of which it may be passed on to others, that slows the process into the shapes of sentences that can be written down.

Because of the telepathic nature, there is no need to wonder whether I am getting the information correctly, or what the other intellect really means; there are no barriers when communicating telepathically, and therefore no means of playing word-games or power-games, nowhere to hide. I have never been given information in 'tongues' or which I cannot understand, though in most cases, there is far more to what is said than appears on the surface. One example of this is taken from the goddess text:

'... the body of the man another to lie beside it on a bed of moss, within the tangled webs of her rainbow hair.'

When I noted this sentence down, I thought it odd, and pondered the descriptive *rainbow*. I thought it must be wrong, it did not seem to make sense. But I never alter anything that is channelled, except when I feel, after careful consideration, that I might have allowed tiredness or lack of concentration to mislead me – even then as little as possible, since the spirits are usually far more accurate than I can ever be. Consequently, I left this particular phrase alone.

It was some years later, when the words had been printed, read, and even recorded, that I suddenly saw, in a flash of insight, that *rainbow hair* referred to the strands of the aura, and that the picture of the man and woman lying with their bodies surrounded by the beautiful subtle shades of the aura, streaming long threads of colour like the unearthly aurora borealis in the northern skies, was far more true, and more graphic than I had imagined.

Going Forward

The spiritual foundations and truths on which we must depend in order to go forward with confidence into the future, will be different for every person. Many of the sitters who have consulted me have felt compelled to make a somewhat defiant statement at the beginning of their session – 'I think you should know that I am a Buddhist', or 'I must tell you that I am a devout Roman Catholic'. Whatever the formal religion or background, however,

128

people often feel that in spite of their faith, there is still a vague, inexplicable sense of something missing. They want to hear more about psychic, mystic or spiritual progress, but are worried that by consulting a psychic or clairvoyant, they might be expected (for whatever kind of sinister reason) to give up that faith. So they make their position clear before the sitting starts.

I often wonder why the general public assumes that a person with psychic powers is unlikely to possess a belief in the Godhead. There is I think an uncertain assumption that psychics themselves want to 'play God' and have already assumed self-appointed divine status. One instance of this was in the remark of a lady who read my book *A Psychic's Casebook* (one must assume it was against her will). After plodding gamely to the end, she declared that she found it uncongenial. 'More miracles than Jesus,' she sniffed scathingly.

If the question ever arises, I tell sitters categorically that 'I am not trying to convert you from or to anything'. We have already seen that to the psychic or mystic, all faiths lead (as cannot be stressed too often) in the same direction, to the same basic truth – it is at this point of awareness that true understanding and spiritual progress can really begin.

The Interpreter

Part of my work as a Wise Woman is to reveal spiritual wisdom to those who come to me seeking food for their souls. This is not arrogance – every blade of grass and flight of a small bird provides the same. Perhaps it would be more accurate to say that I act as an interpreter, that I am familiar with the alphabet of wisdom and the language. And it is certainly true that many people are seeking guidance, rules they can follow, foundations on which they can stand safely as they look into the dawn of tomorrow.

The foundations which appear to be available for us to lean on as we view the new millennium, seem to most people to be worn distressingly thin. Great civilizations have come and gone – the moral and spiritual fibres of the 'Empire' we ourselves are familiar with have been severely strained during the last hundred years or so in the West, and our world is shadowed by dark ugly clouds – never-ending war, greed, the pernicious rather than the beneficial effects of drugs, cynicism, callousness and alternatively-created realities where there are no boundaries of compassion or, seemingly, human decency. Hope and faith, hardly surprisingly, seem to be wearing rather thin.

But the truths which have always been there are still with us. The source never dries up, the words may sound different but the messages are in fact always the same.

In my work as a Wise Woman, I have been given a good deal of channelled or inspired wisdom, some from sources I recognize, such as the Goddess, and others that are not immediately recognizable. The most striking fact to have emerged from this work is that every one, each voice from wherever it has come, has been saying the same thing. Prophets of the past, and of different religions, have passed on, endlessly, over and over, the same messages, the same instructions, the same promises of hope and truth. And now, even on the brink of space, the guidelines are exactly the same as they were in the beginning.

At one stage, I began to receive a quite detailed message which seemed to be from a very ancient civilization. I call it the Notta Manuscript, Notta, their word of greeting, which I translate as 'good will', was the only one which I was given in their 'language'. It was filled with incredible wisdom, but as I progressed, I was rather dismayed to find that it was beginning to sound similar to the Messianic prophecies in the Bible – and one must constantly question whether inspiration is coming from within rather than without. It was only after much thought and investigation that I realized that the whole concept of the Messiah – the

Redeemer, the Inspiration, the Saviour, the Gift, the Light – never began and will never end. There has always been promise of such a one. And of course, there have in the past been many Messiahs. I have met several myself, in the present.

The Notta Manuscript (parts of which I have given elsewhere in this book) is a guide by which to live, a consolation for today, and a promise for tomorrow. It applies equally to all – and we share it with the dwellers on other planes of existence. For the Messiah exists not only to fill a human need. I was also aware of the links with another distant world or planet – I called the inhabitants of that world the 'Formotans' because once again I was given only that one word in their own language from them – and they too lay a claim to their Messiah, explaining their situation in the following words:

The Prophecies

The Formotans tell of their Son

We from a lost and alien world do borrow the lineaments of your faded dreams and the echoes of your flags of war and battle to relate to you the story of our loss and our suffering and of how we were after patience and waiting given a son from without our experience and knowing to take upon himself the sorrows and tears we could not shed and shed them for us.

We cannot say from whence our son was given to us, but that he came, a dark child with light in a nimbus round his head – so to us who were all of light, yet had seen no light that was like the light of our son – and he was always separate and alone and carried within himself the dark and lonely wastes of the land which had sent him. Within him were lonely lakes and pools, dark depths and trees which stood in an everlasting forest and had done so for ever and will be there so long as there is time. And he was

131

the light of our dark days and the first time that we who had no ears ever heard the patterns of laughter and we were given back living because he lived and we do not die as was foretold because he has willed it so.

And yet he is not of us and will never be of us and we who esteem him can not reach out and must only live to prove to him that his dark and fragile light burns yet fiercer than the blinding nucleae of our many suns. He is our sun and we are his, like sparks within his hands though his fingers cannot encompass us or touch us. We are waiting when his spirit is freed for then we can do him honour and galaxies await to conduct that spirit to burn among us gigantically as universes shatter like glass and the rings of time dance each with the other and we can know him at last.

The Notta Manuscript

1

The prophets speak in no more riddles. It is simple. Follow where you are led, having first refused to walk where you are led. Accept, having first fought for the right to refuse to accept. Remain silent, having first given your soul for the right to speak.

Be still, and yet go forward. Listen, when there is nothing to hear. Seek that which you already possess. Shut your eyes lest the light dazzle you. Give when you have nothing to offer. Be there. The time will come, and the place. Know nothing and you shall know all.

2

There is a stairway of rock that leads to the sky. Ascend and wait. Lift your face to the sun. Do not ask why, for you know already within your heart.

Let the fire burn and the smoke rise. Sing the musical note which does not change and let it go on the wind. Do not delude yourselves with the herbs and grasses for they bring the colours of unreason. Reason is pure and has no colour. It is, simply. The being is everything.

3

Keep silent, for in silence is the sound and the song. Speak with your heart and your soul and do not wait for an answer. It is already given. Dream in signs and symbols and portents for they are the only language that endures.

Do not allow your emotions to blind you for they are merely the comfort of children and will be left behind you as you grow. You do not need them for the being is all, and contains everything you will require.

4

There is an enemy and he is nameless and formless and greatly to be respected as an adversary for he is yourself. Know yourself and you will know your enemy and can meet him at the tilting-ground of your own soul and vanquish him so that like the mist in the early morning he will leave you.

Do not fear. Fear is the crying of children in the dark. The dark is empty space. There is nothing to fear.

5

The sleeting snow whips like lashes of the slave masters and the bare feet drip with blood. Groan beneath the yoke no more, for you are freed and the oar of the galley-slave is taken from your hand even as the tatters of skin upon your bare feet are healed. The compassion of your redeemer has no name and cannot be measured, for it is fathomless as the sky and intangible as the wind and fills the earth like the murmuring of doves and the howling of the gale.

Do not try to stand against him for he will defeat you with the weapons of pity and gentleness of heart and understanding that is infinite. The birds surround him and the ants crawl to his feet and the snow melts lest it should touch his hair, such is he.

The worms drag themselves from graves to lie near him and the snails with broken shells will nestle near to the thrush. He is here. The being is enough, the being is enough. Ask for no more.

6

Set no more your face to the past nor to the sweet gardens and ponds of water where life was good. The caravan must move on and all the tears of the weak and the blandishments of the fair will not stop it. He who is among you speaks with gentleness and softly, yet he carries the world upon his shoulders and if he should stoop, you will fall. He asks for so little, he demands nothing, and his hands are empty from giving. One thing only must you do. Turn to him and acknowledge him.

He has trodden the dark places, he has dared the forbidden summits of peaks where even the sky is the colour of rock and there is no sustenance for the body and no hope for the soul. Of his own free will he chose to venture into the void of desolation and because of the sweetness that was within him the void could not hold him, and so let him go.

Where no sound has been heard, he sang and caused green shoots and little flowers to bloom. Where prisoners had languished in their chains so that they were fleshless bones, his touch revived and gave life. He walked defenceless into the tomb and the dark fell back before him and before the light of his eyes.

7

My life was rich and filled with music and feasting and fruits, golden ornaments and flowers and the love of men, until the moment when I saw him. He was nothing and carried a dry stick upon which there were no leaves and no blossoms. He had nothing, and yet he reached out his hand and gave into my keeping the most precious of jewels – his own soul.

Guardian of the flame, the webs of the universe bedeck me, linked by fiery stars, each a knot of knowledge equal to the most refined steel that can pierce hearts black as sin.

8

As the last leaf withers on the tree and the last petal falls from the drooping flower and the land is caught beneath the mantle of winter and life ceases; and as the burial party winds its way with mourning and lamentation to the grave, so life will cease for you, and the sounds of mourning will rise to the still heavens.

The eye will see death, the heart will feel death, but you will see not death but life, not mourning but rejoicing. You shall see not with your eyes but with your hearts, and feel not with your hearts but with your spirits, and all that was familiar shall be strange, and all that was a mystery shall be the only truth you ever knew. You shall rise to the very depths, and be thrown down to stand beside the infinite, your tears shall revive the melancholy and your laughter close the eyes of the dying.

9

There will come a great sandstorm which will cover the land and the sand will whirl and choke and cover up the bodies that do not survive. The sun will be hidden and the moon will seem as blood. The dark figures of scavengers will haunt the earth and there will be no place for righteousness and the reaching out of hands, for all will be seized.

My wrath is all for I know no other.

Rejoice with tears, remove yourself from love and simply exist. Do nothing. The being is all.

10

There is no dark only the dark of the soul, and no scavengers only wraiths conjured by the herbs thrown upon the fire. All else is light, and he who is with you that light. Notta.

Making contact

As every person is to some degree psychic, so the telepathic abilities and channels of alternative communication are present in the same way that the senses of sight, touch, hearing and so on are something most of us take for granted. It is very common for someone to be able to 'read' messages from those close to them with no words being spoken, and how often do we hear: 'I knew exactly what he/she was going to say.' It is only a step further to visualize holding communication with intelligence which exists on some other plane, but which we cannot actually see.

People generally have the wrong idea about communication via the mind. They expect that it will happen as a conversation happens, one voice 'speaks' and another answers. In fact, as I have explained, once the channels of communication are open, actual contact is more likely to occur as a single unloading of information which takes place in the fraction of a second within the mind. Speaking for myself, I generally find that a conversation becomes impossible, as a single word given to me from a source of great wisdom can have the effect of the contents of twenty encyclopaedias unfolding in incredible detail. If I try to ask a brief question, I find that before it has mentally left my mind, the source has given me (in a fraction of a second) an entire rundown on all the significant events of my life and in the development of the universe which have led to that moment of asking, and the answer, which may, as I have said, be only a single word, would take me centuries to explore.

It is my belief that the phenomenon experienced at the point of death, and which has always been associated with drowning (probably because more people survived the drowning process and were able to describe afterwards what had happened to them), the so-called 'complete mental run-through of my life in just a few seconds', 'my life flashing before my eyes', is no more than a communication of the sort I have just described, taking place as the channels open and the soul begins to pass from its confinement within the human condition.

So how does one become adept at communicating intuitively or 'channelling' messages from outside sources?

Communicating and Channelling

How to Begin

Unless you are in the habit of channelling regularly and are familiar with the process, the main problem at the beginning has nothing to do with where the information comes from, whether it is an ancient or alien entity or a departed spirit, or is your Higher Self. It does not matter whether it takes the form of question and answer or turns into an unstoppable lecture by some invisible sage who cannot wait to enlighten you and wants to dictate volumes for you to take down and give to the world. All of these are equally possible.

The stumbling block is the actual communication itself. Making contact is not as simple as some authorities would have us believe, and if you can actually manage to receive anything at all which possesses the authentic feel of truth, that is quite an achievement.

Messages and information must come via any, or all, of the following:

1. The mind, with your awareness.
2. The mind, without your awareness.
3. The hand (or typewriter or WP) consciously.
4. The hand, unconsciously.

Since you want a record of what you receive it will either take the form of writing something and being aware of what you are writing, or writing something without being aware of the message. You may therefore think of what you record before you write it down, or write at random, and see what emerges. So-called automatic writing was much practised at one time. The pencil rests on the paper, the writer shuts his eyes and waits, and the hand moves by spirit guidance. Keep on even if it is just a lot of meaningless squiggles, recommend the authorities. You can try this, but I personally have never seen anyone shut their eyes and produce anything except more and more meaningless squiggles. However, it could be that this method might work exceptionally well for you.

More common is the practice of writing down everything that comes into your head in one long stream of consciousness. Many people produce whole books by this means. Concentration, suspending judgement, not worrying about grammar, spelling or punctuation, or even what the words mean, will certainly produce *something*, and as with anything else, you will find the 'feel' comes with practice.

The ability to link with the sources of wisdom often comes when the person concerned is in trance. Many people are natural mediums, but they are reluctant to explore this gift since the word 'medium' has commonly come to mean some sort of hysterical, bead-jingling crank – a concept encouraged by the intellectually-minded in the press and media today. In fact, if you accept that there is a spiritual plane as well as the physical one we are aware of, it is quite obvious that there is nothing odd about some people being able to link up with both with no trouble. Nobody disputes the claim of a priest of any religion to be in touch with his god.

The word 'medium' means a channel, a way or means. The channel itself does not do anything, it simply allows messages to pass along it.

Try concentrating – without becoming tense or forcing the issue – on a candle flame or softly shining object like a piece of silver jewellery. Gaze into the glow and allow yourself to be drawn within it, an empty space with no will of your own. You may find that you will speak words without being aware of what you are saying, or you will know that you are receiving a message. In this situation, it is important – especially at the beginning – to work with a competent friend who will not only write down what you say, but will act as a control so that you do not find yourself in difficulty. There is no reason, though, to suppose that the process will be 'spooky' or difficult – for apart from the fact that it uses up energy, most people who 'channel' or work as a medium will, I know, agree with me that basically, it is no different from taking dictation in an office.

8

How to Live with Magic

Genuine magic is transformation, is positivity, is joy, which in turn create health and luck. And in this age of 'self-help', many authorities make a point of underlining strongly that we are our own magicians, we can do it all ourselves. We can take charge, creating our own good fortune, for instance, through visualization – picturing what we want and the way we want things to be. Just think of what you want, is the message for today; think of it hard enough, and you make it so. What is more, the tradition of waiting for instructions, waiting to be told what to do, knowing one's place and keeping to it, seems to have gone for ever. We are all equal, and with a few choice hints from a self-help manual we can, single-handedly, effect miraculous cures for our emotional hang-ups, and put everything in our lives in order. Once we have the keys, we can unlock our own doors, we do not need, seemingly, to rely on anyone else.

In many ways, these precepts work. Self-hypnosis, by means of which we can help ourselves to break negative habits, think constructively or tackle the future with assurance, is purely a matter of telling ourselves – in such a way that our mind accepts the instructions – the ways in which we *want* to improve our lives and behaviour patterns. Once we really desire wholeheartedly to take action, and believe we can, our faith can indeed, as the scriptures promise, move mountains. It is all a matter of attitude. If we have no faith in ourselves, we can do nothing, and each little failure only convinces us that we were right to think we would never get anywhere or achieve anything.

But in my experience – as so often happens when people seek out the Wise Woman for advice or help – the mere pointing out of alternative routes, of ways in which there can be a shift in attitude, does help to clear the way for people to perform their own miracles, scale the mountain peaks entirely on their own. The true magician does not just perform dazzling feats and demonstrate that he is very clever. He helps all who consult him to become aware of their own potential, to see the realms of magic that exist alongside the everyday, to realize that these realms are open to everyone and that we are all, in our different ways, dealers in magic and spells.

Days Full of Magic

It may come as something of a surprise to realize that most human beings actually live lives crammed full with pagan (and other) magic practices and rituals. Everything we do is ruled by magic, something that is inherent and automatic, which we practise without thinking because we grew up with it, and which we usually refer to, if we think about it at all, as 'tradition' or 'superstition'. But we do not neces-sarily have any conscious intention of casting spells in order to get what we want for the magic of everyday is prompted by other, more sinister motives.

Basically, the practice of magic springs from two sources – fear and a need to feel that we are in control. These atavis-tic dreads and desires are as old as man himself, and have never been far from the surface of his concerns. Throughout history civilizations have been ruled by the magicians, the augurers, the prophets, the seers, the casters of spells and dispensers of philtres. But the charms, the superstitions, the beliefs, were passed down, mother to daughter, family by family, through every class of society, and provide an invisible text of ancient knowledge which, though often for long-forgotten reasons, is familiar to each of us today as we in our turn, face our own future and what it must hold – our own 'undiscovered country, from whose bourn no traveller returns.'

The origins of magic have their roots in the awareness that there are around us powers and forces greater than ourselves, which we cannot reason with or control. Early cultures did of course conceive the image of powerful gods and goddesses who were responsible for whatever might happen, and indeed of lesser beings such as sprites, imps, demons, elementals, fairies. In the study of magic (in this particular case usually spelt 'Magick') one can find complicated descriptions of all the levels of existence, and lists of the beings which live there, right up to the angels and archangels. Such works as that of Abra-Melin the Mage, which we have already encountered, personal spell-books of early magicians, spend a great deal of time listing the names (those vital *names*) of angels and spirits who can be called upon to assist in working with magic.

Calling upon the name of a deity is perhaps the simplest way of making magical contact. We invoke the protection of a deity constantly, whether through the involuntary 'Good Lord!', 'Heavens above!' or the traditional 'Inshallah' or 'Allah go with you', or 'Vaya con Dios'. We attack the evil forces ranged against us when something goes wrong and we scowl 'Hell!' or 'Damn!' in their direction. All swearing is a form of invocation or magic.

Regarding names, it is interesting to note that the ancient Celts often referred to their gods, as many cultures still do, as nameless – one more example of how names might be too vulnerable or sacred to be mentioned. An ancient Irish ritual phrase was 'I swear by the gods by whom my people swear', giving no name. It is also part of the fairy tale and myth tradition that an evil can best be faced and overcome if it is identified and confronted as itself – by the correct name, as it were. The power of dark magic often springs from secrecy, confusion, misleading information and vagueness. Test this for yourself, and always identify anything that confronts you for what it is. It may be your own fear or doubt, lack of confidence, a feeling a relationship is out of your control. Always, if you see things in perspective and accept what you cannot change, resolving to take action in whatever way you can to improve matters, you will feel better, and lose that sense of helpless dread.

The idea of an all-powerful benevolent deity was not one that found favour with the ancients, for the simple reason that in their view, it did not explain the many terrifying and seemingly random disasters which stalk us through life and can strike out of the blue without warning, at any second. It was obvious, they concluded, that even if there was one benevolent god somewhere, there must be others who, together with their legions of little helpers, were grinning as they nastily waited to pounce, like a cat with a mouse. Simple logic suggested that the best thing to do was to learn to propitiate the dark forces, and so our ancestors set to work to discover all the charms, rituals, amulets and spells they possibly could which might help to keep the dark, the unexpected disaster, the sudden catastrophe, at bay. Magicians trod the dangerous paths into other worlds to find these answers, but the knowledge they uncovered has been in the general possession of all humanity ever since, and except when the human race considers itself 'beyond superstition' – too sophisticated to feel fear, it has been practised constantly.

It is interesting, though, that individuals of great wisdom, workers of some of the most powerful magic possible – and we can perhaps include Jesus himself here – are not usually reported as casting formal spells at all unless they have to – if some dramatic gesture is obviously necessary, for instance. They do not need to carry out rituals or cast spells, for their link with absolute power is direct. In general, the more sounding of drums and flag-waving, the less likelihood that the magic is really powerful. It is as simple and as everyday as putting the right shoe on first when you are getting up in the morning (thus making sure you avoid starting the day with your left – the *sinister* – foot, which is the side where the devil hovers waiting to do you harm, forward.) In case you forget to do this, however – something that can happen to any of us from time to time – it is not advisable to worry too much, for there is also an ancient rule that you must put your left sock or stocking on first, which, by the same reasoning, would presumably give the devil a chance to influence your day. In actual fact, it probably makes no difference whichever you put on first. Strangely, though, left sock first seems to have been a long-established formula for winning the football pools.

Courting Favours

The magic of the people is basically quite simple. Its purpose is twofold: to protect against bad luck – in other words, malevolent spirits or powers which might be hovering suspiciously about, ready to step in and spoil everything – and to ensure that beneficent powers beam down and make good things happen (to draw good luck to the person or place concerned). 'Luck' itself is often no more than the confidence and faith which comes, as we have seen, from a positive attitude and an awareness that we do possess a great deal of control over our present and our future – and also in the way we choose to regard the past. Human beings being what they are, however, it is not surprising to discover that many great achievers of the past seemed to feel the need of magical reassurance.

The supernatural properties of iron have been recognized for centuries. Add the ancient power of cold iron to the traditional mysteries that cling about a horseshoe, used magically for defence, protection – and in passing, to shoe horses. Lord Nelson had obviously heard of the powers of horseshoes, and perhaps as a little extra insurance as he sailed into battle at Trafalgar, he had one nailed to the mast of his ship the *Victory*, and made sure that everybody knew about it. The result was, of course, that the French fleet never stood a chance.

The most unlikely people can be discovered to have been extremely twitchy with regard to superstition and everyday magic. Many eminent brains – Socrates, for instance – were not afraid to admit that they were seriously concerned about provoking the baleful influence of the evil eye. Alexander the Great and Napoleon Bonaparte, who one might imagine had good reason to fear nothing at all, were among the most credulous and timid, luck-wise.

On hearing the solemn prophecy by the priests of the Chaldeans, that his latest victory would kill him off, Alexander tried to outrun this threat of potential death by avoiding further dangerous battles, but in vain. He died simply living peacefully enjoying himself feasting and drinking. Napoleon is still remembered for his *Book of Dreams* and the cards which still carry the name of the psychic he consulted constantly – Madame Normand.

As with all things, there is a middle way between ignoring luck outright and refusing to believe in it, and taking the whole idea to extremes. Some people will deliberately take the opposite course to one which seems to offer a lucky break just to demonstrate that they do not need the assistance of the fates. Others will not take any step at all unless they have checked with their psychic adviser and astrologer. A surprising number of businesses rely heavily on such advice to let them know when the day is an auspicious one and when to take action. This, of course, is exactly how people behaved in Ancient Rome, and Julius Caesar's decision to attend the Senate against all warnings that he would regret it only reassured the ordinary Roman citizen that to disregard the omens, signs and portents was likely to be literally fatal.

I have encountered many people – generally with some psychic power or ability themselves – who become so obsessed with checking their decisions and actions to make sure there is no dark doom hovering if they take any step at all that they will lay out the cards or examine the planetary state of the heavens every day, sometimes several times during the course of twenty-four hours. This cosmic or psychic checking becomes a crutch without which they do not dare to take a single step. The result, however, is simple and drastic. The powers will repeat the same messages for a while, but then they stop. For whatever reason, we must all take on our own responsibilities, and we cannot lean on a celestial voice to make our decisions for us. Even Julius Caesar made the decision to go to the Capitol – and his death – of his own accord and with full awareness of what he was walking into.

Almost every action we take during a day has some magic charm or ritual connected with it which (more often than not) has its roots in the ancient past. And this is just an ordinary day! Solemn, special days (a birthday, a wedding day, a day of death are the obvious few), these are riddled with ritual. However we calculate it, by rise and set of sun, by the appearance of the moon, by a mechanical calendar, every day is a renewal, a fresh beginning, and all new beginnings and rebirths are filled with potential good luck.

There is an especial magic in all the 'firsts' of nature – the first fruits, the first flowers of spring – even the traditional letter to *The Times* reporting the hearing of the first cuckoo. The significance is similar to the reassurance given to the early worshippers of the sun when the steady golden rays were seen at the edge of the horizon after a long, fearful night of watching and waiting – we are safely through the dark, the god has come back to us, we have not been abandoned, he is not angry with us, we are not alone.

Throw On Your Cloak of Magic

It is up to you to swirl your magician's cloak magically about you as you stride through the day. You can become a practising magician with the snap of your fingers. Tingle with power, and impress your friends, as you put some of the most ancient, traditional and effective charms and wise habits into use.

This section is filled with information, hints and advice you can quote imposingly. They are all of proven power and worth. Begin to build up your own personal collection of magical items, and see which way the spirits lead you. Some people will be drawn to healing, others to divination and prophecy. Most of all, enjoy your magic, even while you treat it with respect.

A Wedding Ring possesses deep magical powers both because of what it signifies and because it is (preferably) made of gold. The healing power of gold encompasses the whole body, regenerates the tissues and strengthens the nervous system. It attracts and intensifies love and eases the mind. You may stroke a wedding ring gently on the afflicted area to cure a stye on the eye.

Keep an **Amethyst** near you as a source of power. The purple colour signifies regality and authority.

Pyrite, or Fool's Gold, if placed near a person who has personality difficulties or a fragmented personality, has a unifying effect. When you look at the many facets, glittering at different angles, you will see why. This belief illustrates the conviction of ancient magicians and healers that 'like heals like.' In the same way, plants and colours which resembled parts of the body held the cure for what they seemed to resemble. Red bloodstone, also red chilli are helpful with blood problems, for instance and yellow dock (which looks jaundiced) was seized upon as a cure for jaundice.

Suspend a needle on a piece of thread, holding it between thumb and forefinger, quite still, with your elbow supported on a flat surface. If you have a question to be answered with a *yes* or a *no* – as many questions in this kind of work must be (the spirits cannot always go into detail) – ask your question and wait. Do not move your hand. Sooner or later the needle will begin to turn of its own accord. If it turns clockwise, the answer is *yes*. If it turns counter-clockwise (the Wiccan word is 'widdershins') the answer is *no*.

This method is often used to find objects, pets or people which are lost. It can be carried out over a map of the appropriate area, where directions may be asked for accordingly as to suitable places to find a favourable outcome. The answers in this, as with Horary Astrology – finding lost items through the stars – are simple, but can sometimes still be mystifying. On one occasion, I had mislaid a folder with papers in it amongst the books and general junk of a very crowded room. I consulted an astrologer friend, who gave me the information that it was low down in the south, it was near wood, and near the colours orange and black. Even with this to go on, I could not find it, but when it eventually turned up, it was against a bookcase (wooden) along the south wall, six inches from the floor, and pushed up against an orange plastic carrier with black lettering on it.

On **Monday**, hold a piece of wood in your hand and look at your reflection in a bowl of water. This is the day of the moon and she will help you to improve your intuitive powers. Looking steadily into a bowl of water and waiting for information or clairvoyant images to be given to you is an ancient method of focusing clairvoyance called *scrying*.

A crystal ball or tarot cards can work the same way. Anything which gives you a focus will do.

On **Sunday** at midday, you can work on your spiritual progress and link your body with your spirit by allowing a handkerchief with four knots at the corners to rest on your head.

Protect babies against thunderbolts on a **Thursday**, when Jupiter may be tempted to let fly if he sees an infant crawling or lying on the ground. The child should be passed from hand to hand and prevented from making contact with the earth.

Destroy all hair clippings and nail parings so that they cannot (as representations of your physical self) be used in destructive magic against you. And for added security, never cut your fingernails on a **Friday**.

Whenever possible **ease stress** by stroking a pet or communicating with the animal kingdom. Fish and birds in tanks, aviaries, cages or even sitting on your shoulder, bring a harmonious sense of proportion to your troubles. It is literally guaranteed to reduce stress by just sitting quietly stroking the fur of a cat. Animals give love unconditionally, and they can help you link in to your own sources of love, harmony and healing.

To help cure compulsions wear **kunzite**, which carries lithium and will help to correct compulsive behaviour. Mental and emotional extremes are soothed and calmed, physical compulsiveness controlled. There is a growth of self-respect and an acceptance of yourself as you are. Lepidolite will also assist withdrawal.

Keep green **malachite** near you to ensure a calm and peaceful night's sleep.

Peridot is the Healer's Stone. If you are tired and depleted from too much giving to others, this beautiful stone will renew your energies.

To see the face of your future husband, look into a mirror at midnight on Midsummer Eve. You will see him behind you, looking over your shoulder.

Cross your fingers or touch wood to avert the attention of badly disposed spirits as you contemplate the future. The cross is very potent because of its Christian significance – in fact, crossing fingers can even avert an action which is already laying up bad luck for you, like walking under a ladder. Just cross your fingers as you take the difficult and dangerous steps and all will be well.

Touching wood brings us closer to the Celts. They believed that magic and power lived in trees, and touching wood brings you in contact straight away with the reassuring protection of the spirits and gods which dwell within.

As a further protection, particularly against the evil eye, put out your 'horns', extending your hand with two middle fingers curled back and two outside ones held straight. This will stop the devil in his tracks, should you need to do so, and make sure the evil eye (the nasty negative influence or ill-wishing of someone against you) has no effect.

Wear **jade** to ensure fertility and long life.

Moonstone links you with your deeply hidden feminine depths and with the goddess. **Silver** is the most spiritual of metals and will assist your spiritual development and progress.

Hearth and Home

Many people may feel safer with a fat insurance policy, but our ancestors rested easy in their beds in the awareness that they had protected their hearth and home with the power of magic. If we choose, we can do the same, and know that we are following in a centuries-old tradition.

The foundations of our society have their roots in the hearth and the home – though modern times are rendering many of these traditions obsolete. The Elizabethan household, with the traditional mistletoe ball is still reflected in the sprigs of mistletoe we buy at Christmas today, and it is under the magical white berries the Druids cut ceremonially (so it was reported) with a golden sickle that our festive kisses are exchanged. The mistletoe is magical because, having no root, it fastens itself to trees and grows there. Traditionally it is linked with the oak, which is the most sacred and powerful tree in Druidic lore. So our kisses today are in the shadow of ancient rites.

But the traditional magic of the Elizabethan household has passed from us in other ways. The kirtled housewife might have taken careful note of the way the dust settled as she wielded her birch broom, for example, but it is a different prospect today attempting to find magical signs in the working of the Hoover, and the blazing fire on the hearth has disappeared from many homes to make way for the subtly clanking radiators of the central heating.

But lacking the blazing fire that provided light, warmth and life to the early cave-dwellers, and has ever since been the focal point of any place of dwelling – the mediaeval hall, the manor house, the semi-detached 'lounge' with its 'real flame' gas fire – there is no reason why you may not make your hearth anywhere in your home. Your flame can be a candle – even a small night-light – and this will do just as well as your source of energy, your link with the gods and goddesses of fire. The hearth is where you may invoke or make contact with your own particular house spirit. In Roman times, the hearth was sacred to the domestic gods, the lares and penates. The *lar familiaris* is an ancient deity gathered from your own particular environment, and with the power of your ancestors, something you have built up for yourself from your relation with the land and your place in it. The penates are your own chosen gods which you will consult about any family or household problems. Keep tiny statuettes or images to represent them, and do what the ancient Romans did – if you move, take them along first and let them get settled in so that they can make sure everything proceeds harmoniously.

A Spell to Protect Your Home
Choose a time when, if possible, all the members of the

household can participate. The head of the house (this does not have to be a male) will take charge. You will need, for a fully fledged ceremony, the following: a tortoise, in a box or carefully carried as your totem animal. He (or she) is not required to do anything, but his presence is vital.

Also required: a large number of small pebbles, a large can of water, a small bottle of asafoetida.

Determine the boundaries of your home/garden/ grounds. If it is impossible because of, for instance, living in a flat in a city, actually to follow your boundaries, carry out the ceremony symbolically on a large flat tray of sand or earth, using a cardboard box to represent your home, and allowing space around it.

Led by the head of the house, the group will move clock-wise round the boundaries of garden or grounds, finally completing a rough circle. The tortoise will be carried at the front. His presence represents the protective barrier or testudo which the Roman soldiers formed in battle by lock-ing their shields together, and which resembled the back of a tortoise. This was impregnable, and your totem animal will help create a shield of energy that will hold against all enemies around your house. In addition, the slow pace of the tortoise signifies development of this barrier over a period of time, and it will increase in strength.

Calculate the four points of the compass and as the group passes each point, stop and allow one member to lay out, or if the ground allows, bury in the earth, several pebbles set in a V shape, pointing outwards from your home. These represent the tips of spears and arrows symbolically ready to defend the house and the family. To let potential intrud-ers know exactly how dreadful is the fate awaiting them, one member of the group will at various points let a drop of asafoetida fall. This has the medical property of calming hysteria and overreaction as well as being, in its own trans-lation 'an awful stink'. Intruders or invaders with tempers blazing will be well advised to think again before approaching your house.

One member of the group is responsible for carrying the water, and at every few steps will sprinkle some on the ground to purify the area. At the end of the circuit, the whole group will enter the house by the main (or front) door and close it behind them. Light a red candle and let it burn.

Money Making?

If you are still worried about your finances you can rest assured – for though this ritual does not, perhaps, anticipate huge fortunes coming your way, it can ensure that you do not run out of ready cash. Traditionally, if you keep a newly minted coin in your purse you will save it from becoming empty, and the coin will also draw more money in your direction. It is equally traditional to 'turn your money over' when there is a new (quarter) moon, to bring you financial luck.

The Lady of the Webs
('Lady Luck' in the Celtic tradition)

There was a point at the centre of the world where a dark lady sat clutching in her mittened hands the webs that reached out in either direction. She wore a cloak made from black lace studded with jewels that held the Underworld colours of mauve and ruby, emerald and tawny gold. Her hair was made of black threads that could ensnare the heart of the fiercest warrior with their ebony magic. Her eyes held the glitter of the deep seams of coal which in millions of years would also be blue diamonds, so fascinating that all the riches of ten thousand kings and a thousand thousand princes, carried on the backs of richly gilded elephants and mules with silver hooves and camels with golden eyes and collars could not buy.

She sat and held the webs and all the world waited.

154

The Language of Magic

iv

Secret Names
Many of the Celtic (Welsh, Irish and Scots) names are unfa-
miliar to those who have not been brought up within the
old languages, Welsh and Gaelic, or with an awareness of
the old myths. My name – Dilys – links me, I like to think,
with the ancient world, though it is comparatively modern.
You may (if your numerological charts so indicate, or you
simply like the idea), want to take a Celtic name for yourself. The following sample list indicates briefly what the
names mean, or who the characters were in Celtic legend.

Branwen (*or* **Bronwen***)* White breasted. One of the tales in
the Mabinogion is called Branwen, Daughter of Llyr.
Brigid The pagan Brigid was the Celtic goddess of fire,
inspiration of poets, bards and workers in metal. Later her
attributes became attached to the Christian St Brighid. At
one time the name itself was considered too sacred to use in
everyday speech.

Ceridwen The goddess who represents the face of the Wise
Crone, of the Celtic goddess. She symbolizes the necessary
transformation of everything as it passes through the dark,
and guards the cauldron of inspiration and prophecy.

Deirdre In Irish legend, she is known as Deirdre of the
Sorrows. Her story appears in The Sons of Uisneach, and
has all the dark power of a Greek tragedy.

Eirlys A girl's name meaning early lily, which is the snow-
drop.

Elaine The most famous lady of this name – which is a form
of Helen – died of love for Lancelot, and has been immor-

talized as the Lady of Shalott drifting, beautifully in death, in her barge to Camelot.

Gareth His father was Lot, King of Lothian and Orkney, and he came to King Arthur's court disguised, working as a scullion in the kitchen so that he was given the contemptuous nickname 'Beaumains' (Fair or Dainty Hands). He went on a quest (still disguised) to help the beautiful Lyonors, and was plagued throughout by the annoyance of her sister Lynette, who did not want to accept help from a supposed kitchen lad. Gareth doggedly persisted, overcoming no fewer than four great knights in combat, and eventually marrying Lyonors.

Gereint A royal personage whose adventures can be read in the Mabinogion in the story *Gereint and Enid*.

Olwen A character in the Mabinogion. Her name means white path, or white track, so called because at each step she took, tiny white flowers grew behind her.

Pendragon This was the title used by King Uther, father of King Arthur, and by Arthur himself. From the Welsh for dragon and head it can be translated as Great Leader. Occasionally it has been adopted as a personal name – but it awaits its true owner still. Could you be the one who will dare to claim it?

Vivien (Vivienne) Sometimes claimed to be the Lady of the Lake, who gave Arthur the sword Excalibur. Sometimes identified with the lover of the magician Merlin, who used his own magic to imprison him and keep him in her power. In this respect she represents a wonderful example of the power a woman can wield over the most powerful of men. Also **Vivian**, from a different source, a masculine name.

Yvain(e) Masculine or feminine, the Celtic version of Owen

156

or Owain. Owain was a historical character who can also be found in the Mabinogion in *The Dream of Rhonabwy* where there are many mysterious and powerful images and symbols which represent the struggle between the dark and the light, the progress of the soul.

9

Echoes of a Far Place

We can if we wish, make a journey not within the mind, or within time, but to reach the ancient Celtic world within *place*. We can visit the places where the doors into that kingdom can be found, where we can perhaps, if we are lucky, step through them.

In all the lands where the old Celts lived they have left traces behind, and beneath the world of today that ancient world still remains. Within the British Isles, you can find the Celts in legend, place names, monuments they set up themselves, in music, myths, traditions, even in the shape of mountains and the flowing of streams. The Celts themselves – terrifyingly pagan to us as they seem – have amazing similarities to many of their Celtic descendants of today.

The Ancient Celts

Preoccupied with battles and fighting during the day, sitting at night to feast for long hours, satiating themselves with celebratory carousing – and, it must be admitted, probably drinking themselves insensible – the Celts upheld with dedicated fervour the cult of the body. The fighting men – sworn and bonded warriors all – were impressively physical and easy to identify. Enemy tribes were warned of them with explicit description as to their appearance – and it is almost certain that, confronted with a Celtic band, their hearts would have sunk just a little.

It was the Celtic custom for the warriors to dye their long hair blond with lime, which made it into a thick, rough mane, standing out straight from the head. They grew long drooping moustaches and they ornamented their bodies with heavy golden jewellery. Before a fight they began to move in the rhythms and steps of rituals which worked them up into the trance-like state of blood lust known as *furor* which possessed them so strongly that their bodies burned as though with fever, and cloaks were thrown aside. Mostly, the Celts went into battle naked – and this phenomenon is remarked on in old legends, where the heroes burn so fiercely it takes several applications of ice-water to cool them.

The life of a warrior was restricted, lived on the edge, and the constant threat of death and heightened nervous and emotional states aroused produced intense and intimate relations between the warriors, which led, it is reported, to the common practice of sharing their sexual favours with each other and ousting women. Apart from caring for the children it seems from reports of the Celts of Gaul, for instance, that the women often had no part at all to play in this society of fighting men.

But the women apparently had their revenge, for there are also reports of widespread lesbian activity, and of groups of women who banded together in violent feminist cults who indulged in bacchanalian orgies during which they tore their victims (men, supposedly) into pieces.

Terrifying indeed. The ancient myths even contain accounts of how, after a hard day's fighting, the warriors would fight each other as they sat feasting, on some quite trivial provocation. We might be tempted to dismiss them as just uncivilized barbarians (which, of course, in one way they were) but on the other side of the Celtic coin there loomed always the silent forms of the Druids. Even the sophisticated thinkers of the ancient world were impressed by the Druidic wisdom and power, and mentioned the Druids' ability to 'speak the language of the gods'.

As with any past civilization, though, the ancient Celts must seem alien to us now. Yet if we want to look for that ancient world today, try scratching with an open mind at the surface of the present world of football, sports enthusiasts, and evenings in the pub after the game. Consider, even, the preponderance of heroic figures such as the Gladiators. With the application of a little imagination, perhaps the ancient Celts with their violent energies, physical glory and all-embracing passions are not really so very different from ourselves.

The Ancient Land

Beneath the maps of today, lie the lands of two or three thousand years ago, whose features have blurred over the centuries. But again, the bones of the lands the ancient Celts knew still exist. The surface may have changed, rivers altered their courses, mountains altered their contours, but basically the outline of the land is the same. And you can find that land if you look hard enough.

The old myths of the Celtic countries mention many places, often not known to us, but some, such as Tara, seat of the High Kings in Ireland, and the channel between the coasts of Ireland and Wales, we can recognize – though it is admittedly difficult to look out from the coast of Wales and picture a forest and a mountain plunging through the waves, as observers reported in the story of Branwen, Daughter of Llyr in the Mabinogion.

They sent to ask Branwen, who had been driven, Cinderella-like, to slave for her husband at the whims of his Irish subjects, what such a sight meant, and she answered that it was her brother Bran wading to her rescue with a fleet. Bran was too large to fit into any ship – and there is a fascinating little detail which really makes him an individual to us. Apart from gathering the ships and support of other Welsh leaders to go and rescue his sister from her disgrace, Bran apparently carried all the string musicians on his back. This detail is just as evocative as the fact that Branwen herself, unable to send for help through the usual channels since she was virtually a prisoner, had summoned her brother by means of a starling she tamed and taught to speak, sending it with a letter back to Wales.

Apart from the legends and tales themselves, there are guides and local histories which will give you background information here, but you will need to be your own investigator, following the clues that will lead you to your own particular gates into the Celtic world. It is a journey well worth making.

And such a journey will provide you with unexpected discoveries and riches. For once you begin to search for them, you will find the spirit of the ancient Celts everywhere. They can, for instance, be found almost anywhere in the natural world. They particularly venerated woodlands, streams and springs. Their presence can be felt in mountain water, waterfalls, deep pools. And very strongly and mysteriously at the edge of the sea.

The Sacred Groves

The popular picture of the Druids depicts bearded stalwarts in white robes gathered within the sacred grove where they performed their rites. In fact, whatever the Druids actually did within them (for as we have seen, we do not really know), groves were indeed regarded as magical places, and if you walk in any secluded grove alone even now, you will find that some of the mystery and the magic still lingers. The goddess text gives the following instructions:

And to those who would proceed further into the mysteries, for you is the time of fasting and preparation. Robed in the ceremonial ritual with your feet bare to crush the dew upon the grass and the little flowers, you will walk in the grove in the hour before the dawn, with folded hands, speaking in a low voice or else remaining silent while the shapes of the mystery begin to form within your soul. And you will become afraid for the awareness of the goddess is filled with great terror and awe, and you will seek to leave the place and only the dark beasts who pace in the shadows beside you will bar your path. And you will see the star of the morning burn forth clear and filled with purity, and you will be overcome and fall down upon your knees and curse your weakness. And the next night you will walk again in the grove with the dark beasts beside you in the shadows.

Why were trees and groves so important to the Celts? All nature held the secrets of life and death; the turn of a leaf or the fall of a bird's feather could, to the mind open to the mysteries, reveal the past and the future. The third group which, together with the Druids and the Bards (these more commonly known today) made up the Druid order was the Vates. These were born to their station as shamans and interpreters of signs, portents and wonders. They achieved their powers – as we have previously seen in regard to the shaman – by a life-through-death transformation to new and cosmic consciousness, generally involving (as mentioned in the Celtic mythology) testing, endurance, suffering and pain. Even a person who is given a direct message from God will be found to suffer, often very greatly. The burden of cosmic awareness is difficult to relate to the human condition, and a heavy load to carry.

The Celtic Vates had the powers of reading the secret language of the trees, known as the Oghams, twenty letters which made up the magic alphabet of the wise. In Druidic lore, each tree signifies not just a letter and a name, but also other symbolic qualities – a beast, a bird and so on. Trees were far more to the Celts than just growing things. Like the waters, they were doors to the Otherworld.

The Waters

Sources of springs are particularly sacred and magical. One of the most famous holy wells in Wales is that of St Winefride at Holywell. The story goes that Winefride, a pious girl of noble family, was meditating at home one day while the rest of the household had gone to church, when she was rudely interrupted by Prince Madoc, a loutish suitor madly in love with her and inflamed by her beauty. Disregarding her screams, he pursued her from the house, and in a fury of frustrated passion, went so far as to draw his sword and, as she still tried to escape from him, strike her head from her body. But – wonder of wonders! The place where the martyred girl's head fell immediately gushed forth a spring of crystal water (which, after some feats of engineering on the steep hillside at Holywell, continues to flow to this day).

That in itself was miracle enough, but within a few moments, Winefride's uncle, the flashing-eyed St Beuno, was on the scene and he not only had the presence of mind to put the head back on the dead girl's neck, but did it with such authority that it stayed there, and she was restored to life. In fact, she lived for years afterwards, and carried a scarlet mark round her neck as a reminder of her 'death' – an early example of micro-surgery, perhaps, performed by St Beuno in the nick of time to save her.

Visit the Holy Well of St Winefride and you are back in the Dark Age world of miracles. The shrine, with its protecting walls and flickering candles, softly gleaming green light of the pool into which the blessed water flows, is a hallowed place, a place of centuries of wonders, healing and blessings. But there are many other tiny, unmarked springs to be found on high hills and in valleys – not necessarily in Celtic areas but anywhere where you feel you are in touch with nature and with the gods, or goddesses, of the place. If you seek them out, you will find that a little bubbling flash of water, a stone or two, a few ferns, a flower and some moss damp around the spring, can be just as much of a shrine at which to worship and find the magic of the ancient world.

Any naturally flowing water will give you this sense of communication, particularly, of course, the sea, which was an integral part of much of the Celtic myth and magic.

The Visions

We find our spiritual past, our ancestors, our ancient selves, in the rhythm of words and the shapes of the images which are given to us when we open our minds to the past. We may not know the language, yet somehow we understand.

Within the Sacred Mount

From their nests in the dry sand, dust within and without but the fur soft, though shy—

—waited so long—

—*they pass in procession into the grave where the wonder rises-*

—cannot believe yet it is so—

—*light touching and like a petal miraculous—*

—we are so humble, we are not deserving, we are afraid there may be some mistake, all breath holding we may again lose you—

—*but now the petals opening accepting without fear*
                    WELCOME

The King

Though the ancient Celts had never heard of him, one of the most potent names that recall the magic for us today is that of King Arthur. In the era of Celtic Christianity, which is perhaps what many people think of when they use the word 'Celtic' for its richness, splendour and inspiration, the tales of King Arthur and his Knights, the Round Table and the dedication to the search for the Grail – not to mention the passionate, ill-fated love between Queen Guinevere and Sir Lancelot, the whole doomed to a dark, predestined end – grew out of far more prosaic material.

King Arthur did actually exist, but not as we know him. He was not a king, more likely the nobly-born leader of some tribe, or band of guerilla fighters. It is interesting to remember that the Celts were far more likely, in the west, in Wales, at any rate, to engage in guerilla warfare than in pitched battles – the nature of the land dictated it. You could not, for instance, hold a pitched battle on the slopes of Snowdonia. So in this respect, King Arthur was probably far more Celtic in his actual historical role than the legends have portrayed him. His mark on the pages of history was a list of twelve battles – most of them thought to be in the north or Scotland. Apart from these, nothing is known for certain, though there is an incredibly complex web of tradition and myth.

You can track King Arthur down, however, if you are so minded. A body said to be his was unearthed at Glastonbury (a place of magical association with Joseph of Arimathea, who traditionally brought the Grail to Britain) though this claim has been disproved by forensic investigation. Arthur himself, fatally wounded at Camlann in battle with his own nephew, Mordred (who was also his son, through the mysterious machinations of secret incest) was taken on board a barge draped with mourning, attended by four queens, and disappeared into the mist for ever. There is no grave of Arthur. Nobody knows where he rests. According to tradition, he did not die but sleeps, waiting for the time when he is needed again.

In some cave in the fastnesses of Snowdonia – it is said – he and his knights lie in a tranced slumber, waiting for the sound of the horn to rouse them, and they will come out with their banners and battle flags streaming, ready to fight, as always, injustice and evil. It is a magnificent concept, and possesses spiritual depths far beyond mere legend. Find Arthur wherever you can, following the tales, the traditions, the landmarks which can be visited in different parts of the country – Arthur's Seat at Edinburgh, and the cairn near Bulith Wells in Wales where his hound left its pawprint are only two examples.

The Stones

Popular imagination connects the Druids immediately with Stonehenge, and it is generally believed that it was the Druids who built this monumental circle of stones, but this is not so. It existed long before the Celts began their worship, though who originally constructed it, and others like it, remains a matter for conjecture – one very strong theory among those who accept the existence of other planes of existence and 'alien' intelligence is that it was built by beings from outside this world, this galaxy even, possibly to guide their craft or to assist with navigation in some way.

Many ancient stones, barrows and burial chambers contain secrets which are not immediately apparent today. The rays of the sun will fall on a certain spot at a certain time on a certain day of the year – this is the language the ancients knew and understood, the wonders of their stones can be unlocked if we know the secret.

The Druids certainly used the awesome structures like Stonehenge for their ceremonies, but these are not typically Celtic. The Celts have left other records for us in the form of carved pillars and crosses, which bear the typically Celtic designs of the endless knot and other symbols worked today on 'Celtic' jewellery. One piece of sculpture which is known throughout the world can be found in the

Capitoline Museum in Rome. It depicts 'The Dying Gaul' and is in fact a copy of an original bronze. The warrior we have come to know, naked and in magnificent physical shape, his lime-bleached hair thick and with the typical Celtic moustache, seems more alive as he sits, sprawled yet in control of himself in his death agony, than anyone we might encounter really alive at this moment. The Celts not only lived, they lived passionately and they lived every moment to the full.

In fact, the original statue was one of several set up by a war-leader of Asia Minor who, after desperate effort, managed to check the Celts' martial progress. The group he erected (with grim and hopeful irony) featured numbers of Gauls 'dying and killing themselves'.

The Three, The Voices

We have already seen how magical and sacred was the Celtic number three. Everything of significance in that world happened in triplicate. The goddess in many of her forms was three-aspected or triple-faced. Wicca, which is a religion where the goddess is worshipped, holds to the 'Threefold Law', whereby the good (and the harm) you do in this life will be returned to you three times over.

Among many other 'threes' was the magical concept of the 'threefold death', which signified the subjection to, and overcoming of, death by the elements of fire, air and water, which brought to many characters in Celtic myth, and to many of the visionaries of that race, the great prophetic vision which could be gained only through purification and spiritual refinement through suffering. The shamanic journey also involves being able to withstand the pain of crossing the boundaries of death, and returning to use the knowledge wisely in the world of the living.

Triple-headed images still exist. As we know, the Celts were especially concerned with the head, and a carving or image which had the ability to look three ways at once – into the past, the present and the future, or the three worlds of existence, the upper world, the lower world and the under world – was considered to be particularly magical.

In 'threes' of everything we will get near to the Celts, and we can find them in the triads which represent the verse forms by means of which the bards could learn and remember poems, legends and tales in an age when nothing was written down. They learned everything in 'threes' and sometimes, if the occasion called for it, 'nines', which was just as magical a number, being the multiplying of 'three threes'.

Those ancient Celtic bards have left some of the loveliest and most powerful of verse and poetry as well as legends and tales. We can find something of the world into which we seek to enter even in a translation.

Taliesin

Taliesin, poet and visionary, traditionally gained his powers from the cauldron of the crone Ceridwen. He is said to have journeyed into the Otherworld with Arthur, and also to have held discussions with Merlin. The following poem is from an anonymous manuscript which dates from much later than the time when Taliesin lived (being thirteenth century) but here we can catch the voice of the bard and in this case, of the shamanic knowledge and vision of the man whose name means 'shining brow'.

I am Taliesin. I sing perfect metre

I am Taliesin. I sing perfect metre,
Which will last to the end of the world.
My patron is Elphin . . . .

I know why there is an echo in a hollow;
Why silver gleams; why breath is black; why liver
  is bloody;

Why a cow has horns; why a woman is affectionate;
Why milk is white; why holly is green . . . .

I have been a blue salmon,
I have been a dog, a stag, a roebuck on the mountain,
A stock, a spade, an axe in the hand,
A stallion, a bull, a buck,
A grain which grew on a hill,
I was reaped, and placed in an oven,
I fell to the ground when I was being roasted
And a hen swallowed me.
For nine nights was I in her crop.
I have been dead, I have been alive,
I am Taliesin.

The Spirit

More than anything, the Celts were spectacularly individual, spectacularly themselves, and we can find them in the example of others nearer to our own time who have had the courage of their convictions and have refused to bow to the conventions. The ancient Celts never bowed to anyone – and in the nineteenth century, another Celt, Dr William Price, became one of the most colourful supporters of the Druidic system which had been revived a hundred years previously.

The most vivid picture we have of William Price's activities – perhaps even overshadowing the traditional one of the Druids in the ancient groves at their human sacrifice – is incredibly powerful. On a quiet hillside in South Wales, in the dusk of a winter day, Dr William Price burned the deceased body of his infant, Iesu Grist Price (Jesus Christ Price, Son of God) on a fire in full view of the surrounding populace. At the time, cremation was not legal, but Price had qualified as a doctor at the Royal College of Surgeons, and he was extremely advanced in his medical treatments, being familiar with preventative medicine and homeopathic cures. The fact that the doctor was in his eighties and the baby's mother was only twenty-six (and that Price did not believe in marriage, so little Iesu Grist had been a 'love child') added colour to this already colourful situation, and when Price died at ninety-three after a life of eccentric genius and incident history remembered him bizarrely stalking the streets in his Druidic regalia (white robe, red trousers, fox-skin 'Davy Crockett' hat) carrying a red flag, proceeding to the Rocking Stone in Treforest at noon, and to the breathless attention of an audience of townspeople, addressing himself loudly to the sun.

We will find the true Celtic spirit, perhaps, within ourselves, in what we ourselves stand for, believe in, and continue to strive for. The Celtic quest goes on for ever, and never ends.

10

Rites and Ceremonies

The Celts performed their rituals, intended to keep faith with the mysterious and powerful gods and spirits they perceived in all natural things around them, both to ensure good fortune and as celebration of the cycle of life. Their year was based on the ritual marking of their festivals, as well as personal rites to their own particular and private deities, and special sacrifice or more sensational acts of divine propitiation if the occasion called for it.

The Celtic year is built on a framework of four festivals. The Celtic New Year begins on 31 October/2 November, with the festival of **Samhain**, itself a sort of timeless and magical limbo when the barriers between this life and the supernatural are lowered. 'The veil', as tradition phrases it, 'is very thin'. Old tales of the powerful sexual and licentious nature of this pagan gathering underline the fact that it was basically a period in which chaos was given free rein before nature settled into its orderly progression again, and the build-up of energies during the wild celebration would ensure fertility for crops, animals and the people themselves during the coming year.

The second Celtic festival is **Imbolc** (1 February), which was incorporated by the Christian Church with the Feast of St Brigid; and the third falls on May Day (1 May). This is the famous **Beltane**, night of fire, named for the ancient Celtic god Belenus, and during which the Beltane Fires blaze. They mark the return of the sun, after winter, and the beginning of the Celtic summer. Traditionally, the cattle are driven through the flames for luck, and young men and girls, holding hands, pledge themselves to each other by jumping across the fire.

By Wiccan rule, handfasted couples are united 'for as long as love shall last' – traditionally for a year and a day. After that period they can break the agreement with no hard feelings on either side – or they can decide perhaps to make it more permanent in the legal sense.

The fourth Festival is **Lugnasadh** (1 August), which is connected with the ripening of the crops and harvest.

If you marry in a Register Office, have a baby and register the birth, celebrate a significant birthday or anniversary, attend a funeral – these are legally and culturally the landmarks of our lives today, and there are already prayers and formalities in existence which fulfil the requirements of state and church – whichever church you attend. But there is nothing to stop you from adding further magic and commitment in your own way to mark the milestones on your life's journey, and the journeys of your loved ones.

My own feeling is that a great deal has been lost by letting go of the simplicity and innocence with which candles, fire, flowers, water, lights, starlight and moonlight and all the other sources of natural gifts and rhythms can illuminate and enrich our lives. Sophisticated living reduces them often to part of the interior designer's decor, mere 'atmosphere'. But the difference between sitting in a restaurant that has been decorated to look like a Gothic cathedral, eating steak, with huge candles crookedly burning everywhere in iron sconces – or keeping a vigil, say, in the silence of the pre-dawn on some dark or difficult day with one candle steadily burning, holding the light and the faith to welcome the morning in gratitude and thankfulness, is vast.

The Celts believed in natural magic all about them. It is still there, and you can share in it whenever you like. Use the soft, gentle glow of flames, the lush richness of trees with their sturdy branches (the wands of magicians are made from any type of suitable twig, as are diviners' rods) and their comforting, cushioning leaves. Discover the everyday scents such as pine trees, wild garlic or may-blossom, and feel yourself opening to the earth.

Both the colours and the scents of flowers are gifts which cost nothing. Rose petals and clove spice will make a simple pot-pourri if you stir them together in a shallow dish. Lavender will calm you and help you relax. Use flowers for meditation, for an awareness of the natural treasury around you. Flowers, trees, water and the flames of candles or of fire can be used to heighten the effectiveness of the following prayers and rituals which have been channelled from ancient sources. The words given below have no legal significance, but they will bring stateliness, power, joy and magic to your Day of Days.

Ritual Prayers for Initiations Into Adulthood

Awareness or New Birth of the Soul
(suggested age 13 or upwards)

I feel strongly that the custom in certain tribes and nations (mostly outside the western culture) of marking the passing of the child to the responsibilities of adulthood, do nothing but good. Particularly in the 1990s when youngsters may have lived through a most unchildlike childhood, and see no real prospect of achieving self-respect and a place in a tough world, it is necessary to gain a point of reference, a place at which to start the journey, with some sense of where the journey is realistically heading. Put your own small ceremony together to launch your child into the world, and to demonstrate your pride and faith in him or her. If you have no parents or relatives to do it for you, or you are already an adult seeking your reference point, newly aware and feeling vulnerable and alone, then create your ceremony yourself. You will never be truly alone so long as you have pride and faith in your own self.

One of these blessings was channelled from the goddess and the other from a different high level of spiritual energy. The first is for a young female spirit, the second for a young male, but you are free to use whichever draws you – or even include both.

To the Initiate 1

You are walking through the harrow gate that leads into the realms where others dare not and cannot go. You are disappearing alone in a star-shimmer of light that fades into the darkness and leaves them bereft, while you go forward into the light and become one with it. They fiercely envy you, and they will kill you rather than let you experience what they will never know. Theirs is the web of deceit, yours is the wide expanse of the truth.

Fear not, for the stars are still about your neck, and the jewel shines forth between your breasts. Peace sits upon your hair like radiance, and about you flutters a white dove, with a silver feather in its beak. Take it and wear it with your jewels; and wear too the stones of the earth, your birthright and heritage.

Go forward, Chosen One, and know that your feet are sure, and your path is the straight way that leads to the place where you will at last, rest.

To the Initiate 2

Go forth O soul, on thy journey through the world, wrapped in the mantle of my protection, thrown in the deep blue of midnight round thy shoulders and surrounding thy body with the shield of healing and courage. Thou hast tasted the goblet of the abominations and drunk of the wine of filth, and has held in thy hand the dagger with which to strike the abominator; and thou hast riven him to the heart, and slain the fair temptress, whose white body turned upon the stroke into her true form, and spat and hissed the while it slunk out of the light.

O soul, thou has fought a long and weary battle, and here at my altar thou must rest before thy sword is sharpened and thine eyes are lifted once more to the golden crystal peaks, where the light is amethyst with power and the storms shoot lightning like curses into the black clouds that obscure the sun.

Know here the rest of the blessed and the sleep of the pure in spirit and steadfast in soul. Be aware of the gentle movement of the wings which guard thee, and the love that descends upon thy troubled spirit like precious ointment, like a fountain overflowing so that there is enough and more for all thy needs. Drink deep of the clear water, which is without taint, and close thine eyes beneath the shadow of my wings, and let thy spirit rest. For thou hast earned the crown of the warrior and the dreamless sleep of the innocent and the great.

While thou sleepest, the small creatures will gather in silent homage, to marvel at thy deeds and to send up their uncomprehending prayers for thy presence. Thy name liveth already along the pathway thou hast trodden, and before thee like the sound of a mighty trumpet, rousing the stout-hearted to battle and driving the wicked to hide away in fear.

Go forth and know that I am with thee. I have always been with thee. I was with thee at the beginning, and I will be with thee at the end. This is the word of the goddess. Go forth O soul, and take with thee my blessing, and the sun and the moon to provision thee for thy journey.

Revel for Celebration of Marriage, Commitment, Handfasting or Similar Union

This was channelled in two parts, to be performed in two distinct ceremonies. The places where the Revel is carried out do not really matter, and the time which elapses between the ceremonies is irrelevant. The guidelines given in the text should be followed to some degree, however. The first part acknowledges and celebrates the man – the channelling was from far space, ancient wise ones, beings of light, and there is no feminism there! As the Sun and Moon energies, the Yin-Yang, the Dark-Light, complement and balance each other, so the Male-Female must assume each its proper role. In the second ceremony the woman is given her place of honour in her turn.

The ceremonies are given more or less exactly as they were channelled. Each has its own vibration, its own shape, but you may use them as you please. The meanings may not seem clear, but if you feel instinctively that there is something here for you, do not worry about logic. Love, faith and trust speak in language deeper than words.

Celebration of Union (*first ceremony*)

White blooms for energy, light, knowledge, purity, awareness.

Candles are allowed though the flame is not (no torches) – white or starlight. There may be moonlight. (The ideal time about midnight, indoors.)

All that will affect the senses must be pure.

We will be there to acknowledge our son and recognize his human companion. There is a well-spring of energy that is forming faster and must be dedicated and channelled or else it will destroy.

There may be other celebrations but let them take place apart, this is sacred/private.

The son and his companion will set themselves apart in our presence and we will bestow first of all our blessing. A white flame of energy will form above him to raise the power to a high level.

He will acknowledge our presence by repeating the following – silent messages are not enough. The tongue must be loosened and the spring allowed to flow freely once more.

MAN: I your son am here of my own choice, and come to hear your expressions of pride and your gentle words of sorrow. I have trodden a long path and believed and awaited the day, though it never came. I am here, and I believe this is the day and the hour, and I am waiting. Let me know what I must do and I will do it.

The companion and interpreter will then kneel to receive our message, which will be given.

(The message, received in other channellings is in fact: *Shine, Be.*)

Our son will be told the message, and if he is willing will answer

MAN: I do, I have, I will. *Notta. Escar redelict in formota a lucat.* I hold myself in trust for you, and whatever I must do I will undertake it in pride and in general expediency. I accept this. I open myself as a channel for the flame.

Then the companion will rise and stand behind the son and place her hand upon his shoulder and will repeat

WOMAN: I accept that the flame must continue, and link myself in spirit with you to guard and nurture you so that you may do the work of your elders: and I renounce the things of this world and enter freely into my place, which has been waiting: and I pledge with my human love, respect and endeavour that I will serve you well and faithfully, and will never in this life break the link that binds us: and I will care for you when the battle becomes fierce, and I will tend your wounds and open the way so that when the time comes your soul may be free to go and return whence it came.

This I vow with my heart, which is pure, and my faith, which is turned to the light and does not cease from struggling towards the perfect core of being, and my human love, which will warm you through the icy wastes of this world, where the fires of your own place have burned themselves out.

Then the son will reply to us

MAN: I your son accept the companion you have chosen for me to accompany me in my task, and I freely accept the shackles of her human love and needs and trust, and I pledge to her in your presence that for so long as the bond that binds us shall remain unbroken, I will provide for her the fire and strength of my home, which is much removed from this dead world: and I will honour her for her protection and place my spirit within her keeping, in faith that she will not fail me as the battles rage. I ask her to at all times leave free that which is within, and the rest I freely and in human love give to her.

The companion shall if she is willing answer

WOMAN: I take you and I set you free. Wander the universe and I will guard the silver cord that binds you until the time shall come for me to loosen it.

And you our son shall answer her

MAN: Ask me for nothing, and I will give you all your heart desires.

And she will say

WOMAN: I see you as you are. I ask for no more

And we will thereupon surround both with a ring of light and they shall consider what they have undertaken. Then each shall take a white flower and give it to the other, together with salt and bread for the journey, and they shall drink wine together, at which point we will withdraw from their presence and they make any other celebrations or dedications they desire. When they are ready they will kneel together and our son will pray as he wishes in the new strength and for the journey, and the companion if she wishes may pray also. Blessed be they. And they may return to the world.

180

Celebration of Union (*second ceremony*)

In a rocky place shall they meet and face each other and clasp hands across the time and the space, for this was done before but it must be renewed.

They will assume their ancient guise. That is, the lady will appear in the birdsong and the water, the blasted oak and the rain and the tempest. The other may kneel to speak, for it is necessary that he allow her her place by relinquishing for the moment his own high position.

He must look upon the tempest and the dark chasm and bring to her his strength, and he will make his peace with her in these mighty and everlasting words:

MAN: I have trampled you beneath my feet and stricken you with my right hand and I see you a penitent before me, but I give you my place and restore you to the home from which you have left the hearth empty and the fire cold, in honour and in recognition of your strength. I raise you from your prison and bring you back to your singing birds and sweet blossom and high airs within which you may breathe.

And she will answer

WOMAN: Because I have learned to humble myself beneath your feet, I will let you lead me.

And he will say:

MAN: Will you henceforth lead me?

And she will answer:

WOMAN: I will take you and all who come to me. *Then she will kneel and embrace him and say* Now we are equal. *And she will ask him* Do you consent to be priest to guide and inform me with your wisdom, and to grow old at my right hand in constancy and in the faith, so that we both may find peace?

And if he is willing he will answer

MAN: From my people I bring all and I make my pledge.

And she will answer

WOMAN: I do believe you and I resign my soul to you for you to guard it while I go to arm myself for the battle, and I cannot always be ready so I kneel at your feet and place in you my spirit and my trust, for without you I cannot be, and without me you will be driven from this place. But in faith and in trust as in all joinings, I the lady of this place take you for my priest, and live again because of your coming, and my birds sing and my streams flow and I am fertile and give freely of richness to all, and I honour you.

And he will say

MAN: I have wandered seeking you so that the calm and the wisdom could flow once more and now I am content.

And each will say to the other

MAN *and* WOMAN *(in turn to the other)*: In you is my peace and my strength for the war.

And each will say (in turn to the other):

In you is my resting place.

And each will say (in turn to the other):

Rather will I die here than let you go for you are my salvation.

And each will pledge themself to the other and vow to remain faithful, the lady to the priest and the priest to the lady. And they shall seal their pact in whatever way they think fit. And they must think on the fearful and terrible undertaking they have made and resolve in love and trust to assist each other forward, for each was

182

*previously wounded and so do not have their full strength, but
together they will not fail on this part of the way.*

Birth and Death Ceremonies

Some cultures regard birth as a difficult setting out for the
soul on what may prove to be a painful journey, while
death, for those who believe that there is a coming home
beyond the grave, might seem something to be welcomed,
a cause for joy. They each contain something of both, and
are closely linked since they are gateways through which
the soul enters and leaves this world.

Celebrate a Birth

Welcome the small (or simply the new young) spirit which
has arrived, by bestowing (as in old tales) wishes for the
gifts of beauty, strength, wisdom, happiness. If each person
who bestows their gift wills it enough, the magic will work.
Add flowers, water and the blessings of nature – whatever
feels right and significant to you, and suitable for the child.
The following blessing for a new-born spirit was channelled from the threefold Celtic goddess.

Blessing for a New-Born Spirit

*From the silver plains of tranquillity you have descended through
the gate of bone. In the fruit groves wander now, small spirit, in
virgin purity of the white petals and the sharp scents of orange
and lemon, herbs and box hedge. You have tumbled on the wind
within the sails of the windmill, and the movement of the air is
your laughter.*

*Flowers cluster for your feet and the sharp green of the sala-
mander and snake; belladonna and foxglove lie in wait for your
tongue. O child, you do not know how precious is each moment
and how quickly slip the silver beads from the thread, the Wyrd
which has been woven for you. The drops fall back in shining light
into the water.*

O child, thrice be your welcome and your way be thrice blessed.

O hurry, hurry for life is waiting and the sun of your dawning is already rising towards noon. The shadows fall shorter and the globe spins and the dark waits in the west. O child, you are the heir to all that is beautiful, brave, worthy and true. May you use the years of your life wisely, and walk serene and unafraid.

Meditation at the Time of a Death

Deaths will affect all of us and each person who suffers a loss will react differently – our own personal realities are subtly different from those of others, even of someone close to us. This meditation was channelled from ancient wisdom.

Notta (a form of greeting meaning 'good will'). You must face the prospect ahead of you at this time, which is a dark pool with rocks, the only moving creatures the black birds that devour and eat all flesh. Turn to the past, or any other path, my child, and always they will bring you to the vista of the birds, the black sky and weeping clouds, the still pool.

You will try to escape this ordeal in all the ways you are able, yet when the time is come you will step, trembling, on to the rock, slipping and fearful of the beaks of the birds. The light is lost in their black feathers, the wings rotting, the plumage falling, the eyes eaten out.

Be courageous, child, in whatever way you must.

It is one of the eternal laws that when a human soul steps, fearful and trembling, into the pool, then with a great clacking of wings all the birds will rise, ponderously lifting themselves away from the dark water toward the light. Dark mingles with the snow-birds, the star-birds, in one dazzling cloud of wing and flight. For an instant there is no difference. All are the same. They are always the same.

Everyday Wisdom
Thoughts to Live By

It is surprising, as we have seen, how the same questions crop up day after day, time after time, in our ordinary routine. The following 'words of wisdom' to keep you going are from a highly spiritual source which I call 'Mist' and which has guided me personally through many difficult experiences. I found 'Mist's' wisdom, humour and enlightenment broke through the dark and kept me steady when I needed it most. I share some of it now with you.

Why am I needed?
Even one star would be missed.
There is such a lot of negativity.
That is why you are needed.

I did not know things would be like this.
Did your bird know the cage?

Have I the strength?
You know the dungeon, accept freedom. The dark is no more than the light with pain. You are not alone. Loose the thorn and embrace the rose sweetness. It is all the same.
It hurts.
You need me to teach you that? But what is hurt, only joy gone wrong. Too much joy, perhaps – snow can kill as well as fire. There is nothing wrong unless you make it so.

I feel I have failed in every way possible.
Your feelings are not fact. Just shine, *be*. You reflect like a mirror. The blemishes within are not the mirror itself. Find yourself, reflect, do not look at the debris cluttering the mirror's surface. Hold to the light only. Other reflections are meaningless.

I feel very alone and upset.
Why not? You are alone. But the light is waiting, keep towards it. There is a way out. And you have yourself. Always.

I feel responsible for him/her.
They do not want it. Do not play God. You need compassion

for more worthy causes. Save it. They will not notice the difference.

Please tell me the truth, or show me the way.
These you know. But you do not ask what is within your heart.
No. I don't know what it is.
Do not try to know.
But then what would I do?
Shine. Be.
Is that enough?
Always. There is no always – but always. Keep the light steady and sure.

Am I doing the right thing? I seem to be hurting myself more and more.
In the end it is all the same, and you must reach that end in the best way you can.
All passes. This is an image in the water. The water will flow on. You know this. Be comforted.

For Those Who Seek to Follow the Path

We have already seen that the genuinely 'wise' person, in a spiritual sense, does not choose this difficult role, but is born with it as their destiny. The wisest of all great men and women in the world, of all beliefs, know that it is indeed a path, one which has no end, and which sometimes seems to become more stony and impossible to follow, the further one progresses.

Only you can tell whether, in your private awareness, you know that you have such a destiny, or feel you might have been born for this kind of work. If you are not sure, the following words from ancient wisdom will enlighten you:

It is necessary for the soul to sleep until the time of awakening comes.

186

Do not question the sleeping nor the awakening.
If you are asleep, you will know it.
If you are awakened, you will know it.

The work of a Wise Woman or a Wise Man is carried out without knowing exactly what it is, and from minute to minute, trusting the spiritual world to provide all that may be needed and to give constant guidance. It transcends all human politics, laws and material values. It demands the sacrifice of the ego, the offering of one's life, unconditionally.

Yet I myself, and the few people I know who are similarly situated, would not wish it otherwise. To be born with such a destiny is to be privileged beyond all dreams or ambitions. The struggles along this path are a small price to pay for the treading of it. So for those who are beginning to find that this is where their feet are leading them, the last channelled message from the goddess gives a welcome, an enlightenment and a reassurance.

From the bough, the white berry within your cup. Pearls from the sea-strand upon your brow. The prints of your feet in the sand are centuries old, each tide you walk there anew, the shells grating together.

There are landmarks to make you weep, blurry through the rain. The heart sickens with old griefs, blood on the sword.

You walk in moonlight, in the half-light, on the enchanted strand. No sword can rest once it has been grasped, and the heart must fight on, even if the strand is empty. Fight the waves. This is your domain. You rule the shadows.

Selected Reading List

Anderson, Mary, *Colour Therapy* (The Aquarian Press, 1979)

Berresford Ellis, Peter, *Celtic Inheritance* (Muller, 1985)

Carr-Gomm, Philip, *The Elements of the Druid Tradition* (Element Books, Ltd, 1991)

Causton, Richard, *Nichiren Shoshu Buddhism* (Rider, 1990)

Chadwick, Nora, *The Celts* (Penguin, 1991)

Cowan, Tom, *Shamanism as a Spiritual Practice for Daily Life* (The Crossing Press, Freedom, California, 1996)

Cunningham, Scott, *Cunningham's Encyclopedia of Crystal, Gem & Metal Magic* (Llewellyn, USA, 1993)

Fortune, Dion, *Psychic Self-Defence* (The Aquarian Press, 1988)

Gantz, Jeffrey (trans), *The Mabinogion* (Penguin, 1987)

Gater, Dilys, *A Psychic's Casebook* (Robert Hale, 1995). *Past Lives: Case Histories of Previous Existence* (Robert Hale, 1997)

Goleman, Daniel, Ph.D., *The Meditative Mind* (Thorsons, 1996)

Gray, Miranda, *Beasts of Albion* (Aquarian, 1994)

Gregory, Lady (trans), *Gods and Fighting Men: The Story of the Tuatha De Danaan and of the Fianna of Ireland* (John Murray, London, 1904)

Hay, Louise L., *Colours & Numbers: 1991* (Hay House, Santa Monica CA, 1990)

Herm, Gerhard, *The Celts: The People Who Came Out of the*

Darkness (Weidenfeld and Nicolson, London, 1976)

Horan, Paula, *Abundance Through Reiki* (Lotus Light Publications, Box 325, Twin Lakes, WI 53181)

Lacy, Marie Louise, *Know Yourself Through Colour* (The Aquarian Press, 1989)

Lloyd, D.M. and E.M. (editors), *A Book of Wales* (Collins, 1953)

Matthews, Caitlin, *The Elements of the Goddess* (Element Books, 1989)

Matthews, Caitlin & John, *The Encyclopaedia of Celtic Wisdom* (Element Books Ltd, 1994)

Pennick, Nigel, *The Celtic Oracle* (The Aquarian Press, 1992)

Piggott, Stuart, *The Druids* (Penguin Books, 1977)

Powell, Andrew & Harrison, Graham, *Living Buddhism* (British Museum Publications Ltd, 1989)

Rendel, Peter, *Understanding the Chakras* (The Aquarian Press, 1990)

Robbins, Christopher, *Herbalism, an Introductory Guide* (Parallel Books, 1995)

Rodrigo, Paul, *Numerology Handbook: The Complete Numerological Guide to Successful Everyday Living* (Quantum Books, 1996)

Stewart, R.J., *Celtic Gods, Celtic Goddesses* (Blandford, 1990)

Webster, Graham, *Boudicca: the British Revolt against Rome AD 60* (Batsford Ltd, 1978)